secrets of
super-productivity:

how to **achieve**
amazing
things in your ~~life~~ work life

neen james

First published in 2006

Neen James
PO Box 1764
Doylestown PA
18901 USA

www.neenjames.com

© Neen James 2006

Includes index.
ISBN 0-9769258-0-X

Library of Congress Control Number:
2006902931

Edited by Simone Tregeagle,
Ink Communications, Sydney
Art direction and design by Tania Knight,
Elevator, Sydney

warning

to international readers

Because Neen is an Aussie, this book may contain occasional strange-sounding Aussie terms, and frequent Aussie spellings. So, no, they're not typos, that's really how we talk and spell Down Under...enjoy!

I dedicate this book to four of my favourite little girls,
four future leaders, four future pink lovers,
four girlie girls – Opal, Molly, Madi and Ava –
you mean the world to me.

contents

Acknowledgements 9

Amazing Women Say 11

Introduction 15

Managing Your Career 20

How is Your Career Plan? 21

More Please 28

Job Hunting 33

All About Me 38

Mastering Job Interviews 43

Starting Over 49

Recession-Proof Yourself 53

Managing Your Position 101

Making an Impression 102

Networking 107

Happy Hour 113

Great Team Work 117

Coaches and Mentors 123

Coaching and Counselling 127

Managing Your Work 57

Seventy Minutes That Will Make Your Day 58

Making Time Work For You 64

Desktop Management 68

File It 72

Effective Phoning 77

Email Etiquette 86

Working Well With Others 92

Learning to Share 97

Managing Yourself 131

Make This Your Best Year Ever 132

Go Confidently 136

Choose to Be Happy 140

Kicking Goals 144

Healthy, Wealthy and Wise 148

You Are What You Eat 154

Move It 158

Sleep Tight 163

Money Management 167

Additional Reading & Resources 173

For the
Amazing

People in my life...

They say that writing a book is like giving birth to a child...well I wouldn't know about that...but I do know that it takes an amazing team to help achieve the dream of 'birthing' a book. There are so many people that I love and admire, you know who you are, and to you I say 'thank you'.

Firstly, to the most important person in my life, my husband Andy, whom I love and adore. Your support, generosity, encouragement and belief in me helps me to see that I can achieve anything I put my mind to. You are my world.

My editor and dearest friend Simone, without you this book wouldn't be a reality. Not only for your talented ability to make my words sound fabulous, but it was you who first said, 'I don't want to have to print those articles off your website – for goodness sake, put them in a book!' Well I listened...and I did it. Thank you for believing in this project, even on days when I didn't. You make the world a better place because of your love, enthusiasm and incredible heart – thank you.

Tania, you are so gifted and insightful. You have represented everything I could ever want in this beautiful book design. You are truly amazing to complete this project with so much going on around you. I admire you.

Robyn Henderson, what an amazing chick you are. You are an inspiration, a mentor, a friend and role model for so many. Your impact on authors all over the world will benefit so many generations to come – thank you for being who you are.

To all of the amazing women who took the time to read this book and offer their comments and thoughts – thank you – you are all fabulous.

My most special friends Jeni Sellan – you beautiful soul – and Dave and Annie Crick, you guys are legends – you are the best support crew a girl could ever ask for. Thank you for always being excited about my book – you rock!

To my family, thank you for being part of my journey, being so proud and helping to shape who I am today. Opal, you make me smile. When you grow up I want you to know that your Aunty Neen only wants the best for you. Mum I love you, and thank you for everything.

To all my fabulous American friends, Ted & Eileen - you guys are wonderful. TJ, Christian & Donovan, no matter where I am in the world, you will always have a special place in my heart. Karyn - you are an inspiration, you make me laugh and you are a great shoe shopping friend! Maria, You are the 'World's Best Assistant' - thank you for everything.

Lastly to the Chilli Mud Crab Girls, Em, Carole, Miss Jayne, Cath and Georgie – thank you. I feel blessed to have such special chicks like you in my life. Thank you for dreaming big dreams with me, for believing in me, for making me laugh.

Amazing

Women say…

How to Achieve Amazing Things in Your Worklife is an essential tool for every woman's bedside table. Wake up with a problem and this easy to read book has it covered. A daily dictionary with a help desk feel for today's busy woman.
Lynette Palmen AM – Founder and Managing Director of Women's Network Australia – www.womensnetwork.com.au

Well done. It's a quick read, friendly helpful advice, and very practical. It's also written in a simple and easily readable style. If everyone did all the things you recommend they'd have great lives.
Robyn Pearce – International Productivity Specialist and best-selling author of the '*Getting a grip on* ....' series – www.gettingagripontime.com

I love this book – it is practical, the tips are real, and not 'pie in the sky' stuff that takes a degree to work through. And the best thing is that it translates into every single component of life. It also provides a giggle, I love the tip on sleeping in the nude, and the personal experiences that you have added make it warm, so REAL. This is easy reference, and relevant! You can skim through if you need to and find the sections that you feel you need the most – but you won't be able to just read those, because it's so enticing, you just have to keep reading. Real life, real people, real experience!
Jenni Sellan – National Retail Manager – Virgin Mobile

Love the feel and tone. Very practical and easy to dip in and out of. Great tips and easy to apply.
Candy Tymson CSP – Keynote speaker and Business Educator – www.tymson.com.au

I am truly impressed with this book, Neen James has done a wonderful job of providing a simple, productive and practical formula for anyone wanting to achieve success. The strategies detailed in this book can be adapted to fit anyone at any level and in any industry – from a large organisation to a small business. It is easy to read, relevant and most importantly – achievable. Neen is someone who "walks her talk" and I am certain that anyone who applies her advice and ideas will certainly be able to achieve amazing things!

Kim McGuinness – Managing Director – www.networkcentral.com.au

Congratulations Neen on a valuable resource for EVERY person in the workforce. You have really covered the complete A-Z. Plus I love your networking section. Well done!

Robyn Henderson, Global Networking Specialist – www.networkingtowin.com.au

Awesome! Brilliant! *How to Achieve Amazing Things in Your Work Life* is a book which has an exciting approach with priceless practical strategies which are so relevant for those who never seem to have enough hours in one day. Page after page of valuable information, this book gives you the opportunity to share in Neen's secrets, habits, ideas and instinctive networking practices that have enabled her to build a successful business, network and career. A powerful tool for any company and every person!

Belinda Yabsley – Passenger Car and Diplomatic Sales – Mercedes-Benz Australia – www.belindayabsley.com

Reading this book I found myself thinking, 'A lot of this is fundamental', but you know, it's the fundamentals that are so important. If we forget them then there's almost no point doing the other stuff. There are also some wonderful gems of ideas – sound, practical advice delivered in easily digestible snippets. 'Happy Hour' is great. How often in my time as an employee would that have been invaluable, and as I move from 'a corporation of one' to having a team around me, it's a great technique to take along the way. 'Surround yourself with VIPs' – very inspiring people – is a piece of advice close to my heart, and one of the greatest. By being friends with, and reading about, people who you find inspirational it will enable you to become all you want to be.

Kate Bezar – Publisher – *Dumbo feather, pass it on* – www.dumbofeather.com

A great book to have lying around on your desk for those days you need a little pick me up, inspiration and practical advice. Neen shows you how to be your very best – within yourself and at work. She recognises the importance of being happy, healthy and balanced in order to be productive at work. Full of fantastic tips and inspirational insights on all the key things that matter – everything from diet, exercise, confidence and organisation. You can't help but want to make a change for the better after you've picked up this book. *How to Achieve Amazing Things in Your Work Life* is a must for getting the most out of you, your work and your life!

Donna Jones – Fitness Expert – *Good Medicine* Magazine, Personal trainer and consultant – www.donnajones.com.au

Neen James is such an amazingly, talented bundle of positive energy. When you meet her you can't help but feel great! She's a testament to the valuable advice she gives for today's busy woman. I love this book as it's a simple and quick read. Each bit of advice is given with warmth and understanding and is easy to adapt to, straight away. No lectures, no seminars to spend hours listening to. Just some quick easy tips to follow that will definitely improve the quality of your life.
Kerri Pottharst – World Champion Beach Volley Ball Gold Medalist and International Speaker – www.kerripottharst.com

When Neen James 'the Pocket-Rocket' speaks – you listen. Neen James has a personality and drive which 'leaps' out from the pages of her book. *How to Achieve Amazing Things in Your Work LIfe* could only be written by someone who has done – just that!
Claudia Keech – Founder and CEO – www.motherinc.com.au

Introduction

Do you feel like you can never get it all done?

Do you feel like you don't have enough hours in your day?

Do you believe there is no such thing as 'balance'?

Do you feel like your 'to do' list is never ending?

Then you need to stop being so busy and start achieving.

What's the difference?

Super-productivity is not about time management.
It's not about working longer hours.
It's not about investing a lot of money.
It's not about creating more lists.
It's not about crossing things off your lists.
It's not about putting your lists in a certain order.
It's not about doing more.

It is about doing less of the things that don't make any difference, more of the things that create impact – and being able to tell which is which!

Technology has made the speed with which work can happen inconceivably fast. Even if you've only been in the workforce for the past ten years, you'll remember how things that once had to be faxed, posted and couriered can now be delivered instantly by email. And of course timeframes and deadlines have shrunk in response.

At the same time, budgets, staffing and resources seem to be shrinking every year, which means we're working faster than ever and expected to achieve more with less than ever. Is it any wonder that our 'to do' lists can strike fear in our hearts?

There once was a time when it was considered 'inappropriate' to talk about how overloaded, busy and stressed you were at work, but these days it's the standard topic of conversation, ask anyone and they'll tell you how 'flat-out' they are and what a 'crazy time' they're having at the office. The trouble is that it never stops and we are giving more of ourselves – more of our time, more of our energy, more of our attention, more of our health – to work that will never end and never 'settle down'.

It's a new era of work, and the tools that have served us up until now are no longer valid. It's time for a new approach to time.

Super-productivity is about making time

Most of us will have done some form of 'time management' program where we learnt about setting priorities, daily 'to do's and so on. But what happens when you have to start rating your priorities as AAA, AA and A, rather than A, B, and C, like they showed you? Or when it takes longer to administer your 'to do' list than to actually do most of the tasks on it? Or when your 'to do' list gets carried over week after week, month after month?

The unspoken truth is that we never will get around to doing everything on that 'to do' list, and the only things that really get our attention are the ones that scream the loudest. It's time we threw our 'to do' lists away, stopped trying to manage time and started to learn how to make time.

Super-productivity is not about working more, it's about getting more impact out of every hour that you work. It's about identifying those things that will really pay off, spending your time on them, and being prepared to write-off those things that just don't matter.

It's about deliberately and consciously choosing where to invest your limited resources – your time, your attention and your energy – to achieve the outcomes you are responsible for. It's just like any other type of investment, you have limited resources to invest and your job is the get the greatest return on your investment.

It's about getting into it, getting on with it and getting around to it.

This book has been designed to help you bring the thinking of super-productivity into your work life – so that you start to focus your time, attention and energy in the places that will deliver the best results for you. It's jam-packed full of tips to get you started in four areas of your work life: managing your career, managing your position, managing your work and managing yourself.

It hasn't been designed with the thought in mind that you will actually sit and read it cover to cover, I know you're far too busy for that, instead it's designed as a book that you can pick up, open to any page and grab a super-productivity tip that you can incorporate into your life. And, it's designed to be a fabulously gorgeous book because I figure if we're going to be talking about work and productivity (let's face it, wouldn't we all rather be doing something else) then we might as well do it in a glamorous way!

I know that with these tips for super-productivity you can achieve amazing things in your work life.

Shoot for the stars!

Neen James

Shoot for the stars!

neen james

managing your
career

How is Your Career Plan?

It's easy to allow each year to unfold and not give a lot of thought to where we're going in our careers. We get so caught up in our 'busyness' that we don't spend time reviewing and planning our next career move. At school we receive a report card at the end of each year outlining what we achieved and identifying areas for improvement – and, we move up a level every year. We need to treat our careers in the same way – reviewing our progress, identifying areas for growth and stepping up a level, rather than repeating the same year's worth of experience again and again. Take some time to review these tips and identify how you can get your career back on track for success.

Review yourself.

Set aside just one hour every six months to check in on how your working life is going – you might review your achievements, the things you're finding challenging, whether your working relationships are going well, whether you're learning and growing, your salary and benefits, how much time you are spending at the office, how much time you spend travelling for work, whether you're taking your holidays and so on. Think about every aspect of your working life and include it in your review.

Create a career plan.

Create an annual career development plan. Your plan might include goals relating to your remuneration, skills development, mentors, networking, education and so on. Make a list of ten career goals that you want to achieve this year.

Make it visible.

Place your development plan where you can see it and read it once a day to keep you on track and to remind you of what is important to you. This will also help you to eliminate activities that are not productive in helping you to achieve your career goals.

Set financial goals.

Think about your financial opportunities – your salary, superannuation, commissions and special bonuses you could receive. I set a goal to have my employer pay for me to travel overseas – and I achieved it several times! Think big! Consider trading dollars for additional time off if you enjoy travel, ask your employer to cover child-minding services instead of paying your monthly commissions. Be creative with your remuneration arrangements.

Interview your seniors.

I don't mean at the aged care facility (although they would have a wealth of advice and wisdom for you), I mean those in senior positions to you. If you are keen to 'climb the corporate ladder' make time to interview three people in senior positions this year. Ask them how they got there, what they studied, what they read, what networks they belong to and who was important in their career progression. These questions will give you an insight into how to develop the best plan to get ahead.

Develop two new skills each year.

Make it a priority to develop at least two new skills each year – that's only one every six months, surely you can make time for that. If you have foreign-speaking clients, learn a language. If you want to build your internal profile, learn how to write for the internal newsletter. Find skills you can apply to your everyday life too.

Multi-skill.

If you work for an organisation, make a commitment to spending some time in one other department every six months. For example, if you are in sales, spend time in accounting to understand what is important to them when you do your job. They will value your interest and treat you with a new level of respect.

Read four professional books this year.

This might seem like a stretch for those of you who don't like to read, but it's only one every three months! Staying on top of the latest thinking in your field is a good conversation topic for all that networking you are going to be doing and it gives you something to discuss with your senior management when you interview them.

Request testimonials.

Ask clients or colleagues that you have worked with to write a testimonial for you that speaks about your level of service and performance. Most people are happy to oblige, make it easy for them and suggest that they write an email that you can put on their letterhead and have them sign. In some cases, they may even ask you to write it for them! Make sure you do it and keep it on file.

Create a 'Fuzzy File'.

The name of this file comes from my good friend Ron Tacchi. This is where you store all your client testimonials, thank you cards and letters of appreciation. It is great to pull this file out occasionally and read all the nice things people have said about you.

Collect data for your annual review.

If you work in an organisation, each year you will be part of an annual review or appraisal. Be prepared for it. If you work for yourself, still make the time to review your progress each year. As part of your review you should collect client and peer testimonials, certificates for courses you have attended and copies of articles you have had published. When I worked in the corporate world, I always completed all the necessary paperwork for my review (that is, the forms my boss was supposed to complete). I was also equipped with thank you cards, testimonials and so on, and I gave myself an overall rating. This might seem a little too forward, even cocky, true – but nine times out of ten my boss was appreciative and used my comments and rating for the final decision!

Get an accountability partner.

Ask someone you trust to help you with your plan. Outline your goals and ask them to check in on you occasionally. I do this in many aspects of my life and I find people are very willing to help. Knowing that someone is going to check in on you makes you more determined to complete your goals and activities.

Review your industry.

Make time each year to also review where your industry is heading. Is it growing? What opportunities exist? What types of clients are out there? You may find yourself in a very mature, or even declining industry, if so, decide whether you want to continue and if you don't, begin designing your exit strategy.

To team or not to team?

If you are part of a team, make time each year to get everyone together to also work on a team career development plan. Spend time doing a SWOT analysis of the whole team; determine how each member can achieve their own goals within the team. If you work alone, consider what teams you are part of – for example with your clients, church or university. Determine how you can work with others to help them achieve their goals while you achieve your career plan.

More Please

How many people do you know that think they deserve a raise, but are too scared to ask?
You might even be one of those people yourself!
Why is it that we are so afraid to ask for what we believe we are worth? It's time to stop worrying and start asking but before you charge into your boss's office, give yourself the best chance of success by preparing a convincing case.

Do an audit.

Make a list of your achievements in your current role, think about where you add value to your organisation and how you have helped the business to grow. List both demonstrable results such as sales figures, client testimonials and reports as well as those things that can be a little more difficult to quantify, such as improvements in staff morale.

Know what you're worth.

Find out how much similar jobs are paying, look at both your own industry and others to determine what your market value is and what type of additional package benefits are on offer for similar roles.

Create your ideal package.

Make a list of everything you would like to receive in salary, car allowance, superannuation, time off and other benefits. Look at the total dollar value of the package rather than just focusing on individual components.

Consider the organisation's situation.

Be aware of how the organisation is performing before you approach your manager. If times are tough, your proposal might be less likely to be considered but if the company is performing well your manager might be more open to your request.

Book a time.

Make an appointment with your manager and let him or her know that the subject will be your remuneration package. Try to schedule the meeting for early in the day so that your manager is not distracted by competing priorities and you don't spend a nervous day waiting for the appointment time.

Practice.

Go over your presentation in your mind and perhaps even with a friend or colleague. Know what it is that you want to say and why you believe you deserve this raise.

Objection!

List all of your manager's potential objections and think about how you will respond to them if they come up.

Be calm and positive.

Take a few deep breaths before the meeting and remind yourself of why you deserve this raise and the positive impact that it will have on your life. Don't approach the meeting timidly, you have to demonstrate that you are worth the raise – believe in yourself, your achievements, and your value.

Be aware of body language.

Sit forward in your chair, make eye contact and smile. Try to appear relaxed and comfortable not nervous and fidgety.

Build your case.

Before you launch into your presentation about what you want and why you deserve it, ask your manager these questions:

- How do you feel I have been performing over the past few months?
- Do you agree that I have added value/sales/benefits to the organisation?

Your manager's responses will help you to understand what his or her opinion of your performance is and how you should best position your request.

Be assertive.

Use assertive, not aggressive, language when you are making your case and don't moan or complain. Talk about the benefits to the company and to you.

Don't blink, don't look away.

When you do tell your manager the total package figure you would like to receive, don't blink and don't look away. Hold their gaze and remain calm.

Allow your manager to respond.

Remember, you've been thinking about this and putting together your proposal for some time but this is the first your manager has heard about it, give him or her time to respond and process your request. Don't interrupt while they are responding, let them talk through their thoughts and issues and don't try to fill any silences with further explanation or justification.

Be flexible.

If appropriate, let your manager know that you are prepared to be flexible in how the raise is provided to you, perhaps it could be phased-in, include a bonus or one-off payment or involve changing the structure of your current package.

Agree on a response timeframe.

If your manager can't give you an answer immediately, agree on a timeframe within which he or she will come back to you. Around one-week would be an appropriate amount of time.

Job Hunting

Most of us spend more than eight hours every day during the week at work – so when we don't enjoy our work or the place we work, we've got a big problem! It's important that this part of your life makes you happy. If it doesn't, it's time to make a change. I know that's easier said than done and that job hunting is challenging, confronting and time consuming, but if you are unhappy at work that means you are unhappy for a very large proportion of your life. Here are some tips to get you on the path to that new job sooner.

Identify what you don't like.

This can be quite an eye opener and requires you to get out of that general feeling of unhappiness and into the specifics. Make a list of things that you aren't happy with in your current job. Then go through the list and assess whether they are within your control or not. If they are within your control, decide whether you want to change them and whether it would be worthwhile to make the effort. If they are not within your control, that gives you a good indication as to whether there's anything you can do to improve your current situation.

Educate yourself.

Whether you decide to stay or to start job-hunting, make sure that you have the skills and knowledge required to fulfill your job or a new role. If not, look for training and education opportunities and get yourself skilled-up. If you're interested in moving into a new field find out what new skills you require and register for courses.

Ask around.

Identify companies that you would like to work for and speak with people who already work there. Find out who your manager would be and call him or her to introduce yourself and ask whether you can buy them a coffee, as you are interested in knowing more about the company. Create a list of things you want to know about the company, the roles, the recruitment process and so on. This is not a job interview and there may not even be any positions available, you are simply investigating the company. You might indicate your interest in working there but you mustn't ask for a job. If you like the sound of the company, keep in touch and ask the manager to let you know if any roles become available that you might be suitable for.

Interview people.

Find people who are in similar roles to the ones that you are interested in and ask them out for a coffee to talk about their company and role. Find out what they are responsible for day-to-day, what their manager's style is, what they enjoy about the role, what they don't like about it, who their key stakeholders are and so on. This is a great way to get a thorough understanding of what a role or an organisation might be like.

Brush up on your interview skills.

Especially if it's been a while since your last job interview, read books, ask colleagues and friends for tips and be prepared to answer some standard interview questions, such as:

- What three things are you best at?
- What are your key strengths?
- What do you think your areas for development are (in other words what are you not very good at)?
- Why should we employ you for this role?
- How do you handle difficult customers/colleagues/situations?
- How would the company benefit from employing you?

Check your image.

Right or wrong, first impressions and the way you present yourself are vital in people's assessment of you. Invest in spending time with an image consultant, look at the type of clothing and colours you wear, your hairstyle and accessories and make sure you are projecting the right image for the person you are and the role you want.

Be confident.

An interview is a sale, it is vital that you appear confident in your own abilities and are able to answer questions succinctly…if you aren't convinced of your own ability to perform a role, how can you ever hope to convince people whom you have never met before that you are the right person for the job?

All About Me

Your resume is your sales brochure;
it tells the world about your achievements and
capabilities. It should be able to stand alone and
represent you well. When employers are recruiting
they might receive hundreds of resumes...so how
can you ensure that yours is among the short list?
These valuable tips are a good place to start in
creating your winning resume.

Make a great first impression.

Create a captivating covering letter, use friendly language, refer to the job advertised and allow some of your personality to show through. Check and double-check that you have the details of the position and contact person correct. There is plenty of opportunity for mix-ups, especially when you are applying for a number of different positions – but a covering letter that doesn't have the details correct will go straight into the 'no' pile, no matter how suitable you might otherwise be for the role.

Don't present it in plastic folders.

These are bulky and expensive and your interviewer will discard the unsuccessful applications anyway.

Keep it short.

No more than two to three pages maximum. Only refer to the past ten to fifteen years' experience, regardless of how long you have been working.

Keep it relevant.

Only include details that are significant and relevant to the particular position you are applying for.

Start with a statement.

A personal capability statement is two or three sentences or bullet points that hone in on what you are good at and what your special skills and knowledge are. Put this at the very top of your resume so that it is the first thing people see.

Contacts.

Put your contact details in the footer of the document – this will be helpful in case the pages become separated.

Keep it simple.

Stick to a clean, simple layout – this is not the time to start using fancy formatting. Don't use italics or underlining, as these can make reading difficult. Use a common 12-point typeface such as Times New Roman or Arial. Avoid using less common typefaces that may not translate when emailing. Make good use of white space and don't cramp your document – it will be more visually appealing, easier to read and it gives the interviewer space to write notes. Unless you work in design or a related field don't use gimmicks or present your resume as a PowerPoint presentation – interviewers generally don't like this. Keep it simple and easy to read.

Avoid jargon and acronyms.

If you must use acronyms always provide an explanation of what they mean – not everyone is familiar with all the terms.

Talk about achievements.

Talk about what you were responsible for and what you achieved in your previous positions – don't just list job descriptions or bore your reader with everything you've ever done. Put yourself in the shoes of your interviewer and ask 'What does this person need to know in order to make a decision?'

Be specific.

Where possible use statistics, testimonials and targeted information to demonstrate your achievements, for example, 'I was successful in increasing sales by 21 per cent... achieved 97 per cent on customer satisfaction survey', and so on.

Use positive and energetic language.

Try to make it interesting for people to read and easy for them to find the information they need to recognise that you are the best candidate for the role. Avoid clichés and look for creative (but simple) ways to say what you want to say.

Don't send anything!

Unless you've been specifically asked to, don't send academic transcripts, work samples or any other inclusions with your resume, save these for the face-to-face interview.

Get it edited.

Pay a professional to edit your resume and check for spelling and grammar. This small cost may make all the difference between getting your message across and ending up in the 'no' pile.

Ask for feedback.

Get feedback on your resume from people who understand them – don't rely on your mum or best friend for their opinion – ask a human resources professional, recruitment agent or someone that you know who has been involved in assessing resumes and recruiting staff.

Mastering Job Interviews

I've heard it said, in fact it was probably me
that said it – there are few things in professional life
more excruciating than job interviews – they are truly
awful! Throughout my career I have attended many
and conducted many more and the fact is whether
you are the candidate or the interviewer,
job interviews are challenging, confronting and
difficult. You can learn to not only survive them but
also become a masterful interviewee by developing
an understanding of what it is the interviewer
needs and learning to conduct yourself with clarity
and confidence.

Do your homework.

Research the company before the interview – look at its website, pick up a copy of its annual report and ask friends and colleagues what they know about the organisation. It is inexcusable to front up for a job interview not knowing anything about the company and you'll never convince anyone that they should employ you if you don't even have a general knowledge about the organisation you'd be working for.

Be prepared.

Sound too obvious? You'd be surprised how many people don't get this part right. Make a detailed list of all the information you need about your interview, including:

- The position you are applying for.
- The company you are interviewing with.
- The time of your interview.
- The name and position title of the person you are meeting.
- The correct pronunciation of the interviewer's name.
- The approximate length of time the interview is expected to take.
- Directions to the venue.

Know the style of interview.

When you make the appointment, ask what format the interview will take – is it one-on-one? A panel interview? A group assessment activity? Will it include any testing? Knowing the style of interview in advance will help you to be better prepared and save you from the surprise of an interview format that is different to what you were anticipating.

Plan for delays.

If you plan to travel by public transport allow extra time in case of delays. If you are driving, allow extra time in case of delays. If you are walking, allow extra time in case of delays – no matter how you plan to get there, allow extra time in case of delays. There are few worse ways to start an interview than to arrive late and feeling flustered.

Dress appropriately.

Different workplaces and professions expect different styles of dress. Understand what is appropriate for the type of position and organisation you are interviewing for and err on the side of conservative. Don't wear too much make up, jewellery, perfume or aftershave.

Good first impressions.

When you meet the person (or people) who will be interviewing you, look them in the eye, smile and greet them with a firm (not too hard) handshake. If you aren't used to shaking hands or don't know how to shake hands properly, learn. Concentrate on projecting a pleasant, relaxed, confident image. Smile and be personable throughout the interview – you may feel nervous or even scared…but don't let it show.

Be conscious of your body language.

Don't fidget, fold your arms, wave your hands about or lean back on your chair…it's just like your mother always told you!

Name drop.

Address your interviewer by name frequently throughout the interview – people love the sound of their own names.

Listen intently.

Give the interviewer your full attention when he or she is speaking. This will help you answer their questions accurately and demonstrate that you are interested in the role and have a good grasp of common courtesy and professional behaviour.

Be a STAR.

Most interviewers use a competency-based interview technique and many believe that your past behaviour will predict your future behaviour so they ask questions to help them understand what your past behaviours have been. Make it easy on your interviewers by formulating your responses using the STAR technique:

S – Situation
T – Task
A – Action
R – Result

Always try to respond the following way: 'The situation or task was …, the action I took was … and the result was...' Avoid speculative answers such as, 'I would do….in that situation', interviewers want specific examples of situations you have been in, not hypotheticals.

Be positive.

Use positive, lively language. Act as though you already have the role – use phrases such as, 'When I am in the role', 'When I start the job' and 'When I begin working with you'.

Take notes.

Let the interviewer know that you will be writing notes as you discuss the role. This will help you to remember details after you leave and it gives you something to do to stop your hands from fidgeting (it can help to settle the nerves a little too). Make sure that you use a good pen, if you can't afford one, borrow one, it is important to make a good impression and these small details can have an impact.

Know the content of your resume well.

The interviewer is likely to refer to your resume – make sure you know it intimately and can answer questions about all your past roles, responsibilities and achievements. Also, know the timeline of your employment history well; it'll sound like you're trying to cover something up if you stumble over your own career chronology. Take additional copies of your resume with you – one for yourself and another for your interviewer should they need it.

Ask questions.

An interview is an exchange – you are getting to know the people and the organisation you might be working with as much as they are getting to know you. Make the interview interactive by asking questions in response to theirs and at the end of the interview ask any questions that have not yet been addressed. Always have questions ready to ask, you won't convince anyone that you really want to work for their organisation if you don't seem interested in learning all about it.

Send a note.

Take a few minutes to write a handwritten thank you note to your interviewer and send it the same day. It will arrive quite unexpectedly and help to seal your interviewer's good impression of you as well as help you to stand out from the other candidates

Starting Over

These days, people are much more likely to change jobs and even careers a number of times. But we aren't always in control of when we make the change – it's increasingly common that we may experience retrenchments, redundancies and closures. Having confidence in your skills, experience and ability to deal with the challenges of starting over can give you a greater sense of security no matter what life brings your way. If you find yourself having to start over again, try some of these strategies to help get you back on track fast.

Get support.

Surround yourself with family and friends and let them know what's happening. Stay in contact with those you care about and continue your usual social activities. Although you might not feel like it, now is not the time to stop seeing people. Your support crew will help you to stay motivated and positive and they'll keep their eyes open for opportunities for you too.

It's not about you.

Redundancy is now a common term and an accepted part of modern working life, it's not a reflection of you or anything you need to feel ashamed about.

Set up a HQ.

Create an environment that is conducive to your job-search project. Set up a basic office at home that includes access to a phone, stationery, postage supplies, computer and printer. If you have small children keep them out of this area and make sure that they don't answer the phone while you are job searching.

Make a great impression.

Create a captivating covering letter and a winning resume that gives a detailed description of your past achievements.

Get out.

Become involved in local networks and community events, this is a great way to meet new people, make new contacts and find out about jobs that are available in your local area.

Mind your language.

Avoid using negative language to describe your situation, such as 'unemployed', 'on the dole' or 'I can't find a job' and replace it with positive perspectives such as 'I will find a job suitable for me'.

Stay well presented.

It only takes seven-seconds to make a first impression. Make the most of your seven-seconds by smiling when you greet someone, investing in a good suit (if you don't have one, borrow one for interviews), polishing your shoes and making sure that your hair is clean and tidy. It's easy to get out of the good grooming habit when you don't have to do it every day. Remember how important it is both to your self-esteem as well as to people's first impressions of you.

Stay motivated.

Finding a new job is hard work, treat it as you would any work assignment – your full-time job is finding a new role that you will enjoy. Just as with any job it can be frustrating and especially disappointing when you receive 'rejection' letters. Prepare yourself for the fact that you will receive these, they are not personal. Focus on keeping your goals in mind and remind yourself constantly that there is a role out there just for you, it's only a matter of time until you find it.

Recession-Proof Yourself

One of the only constants in our lives is change! The way we live and work is always changing and the challenge is to keep up with the pace and be ready for anything. With some forward planning and an awareness that things might not always be the way they are today, you can recession-proof your career.

Keep your resume up-to-date.

It's so much easier to work on your resume when you don't need it. Review it at least a couple of times each year to make sure that you're ready to respond quickly to opportunities.

Be aware.

Keep abreast of trends, events and issues within your industry. Read professional or trade journals, join industry associations and attend functions. Stay well informed about the world around you through mainstream media and subscribe to relevant newsletters and websites to keep your knowledge current.

Become technology savvy.

Learn how to use technology – don't be frightened by computers, the Internet, email or hand-held devices. Learn how to create documents, spreadsheets and presentations using popular software programs. These skills are transferable anywhere you go and are fundamental to most roles.

Keep learning.

Know which skills you want to develop or increase and look for courses you can attend. Identify how you'll apply these new skills when you return to the office and share the information with your colleagues to increase the value to your organisation of it funding your education.

Be the best at what you do.

Strive to become indispensable in your current role. Learn everything that you can and be the best you can be. Go beyond others' expectations every time, deliver more than you promise to your boss, your customers, your staff and your colleagues.

Become a confident presenter.

Make sure you feel confident in meetings and are able to communicate clearly and comfortably whether it's in a one-on-one situation or to a room full of people. Enrolling in Toastmasters or doing a presentation skills course can increase your confidence.

Know what you're good at.

Write down everything you are very good at. Focus on these strengths and be proud of your skills. Review your achievements regularly and remind yourself that you are doing a great job.

Promote yourself.

Let others know what you are working on and show your manager the complimentary feedback you receive from customers or colleagues – be brave and start telling people about your achievements.

Relax.

Enjoying a happy and well-rounded life is vital, it's not all about work and in fact you'll perform better at work when you have other interests that help you to recharge and stay fresh. Make it a priority to spend time on other things in life – take up a hobby, join a sporting team, catch up with friends, get away for the weekend and fill your life with fun.

managing your
work

Seventy Minutes That Will Make Your Day

How you spend the first 60 minutes and the last ten minutes of your day will affect your productivity and achievements – all day. Most people launch into the day without a second thought; we arrive at the office, unbundle our bags, grab a coffee and start responding to telephones, emails and colleagues – often all at the same time. It's hardly surprising that most people feel like their days are out of control as they fly from one task to the next, and when there is a lull in the excitement – they wonder what to do. It's an exhausting, unsatisfying and unproductive way to work. Even if you are in a position where you need to respond to many demands, investing in the first 60 minutes will pay dividends all day long and just ten minutes at the end of the day will set you up for the next. If you've ever left the office wondering where the day went or how you could be so busy without achieving anything, try this...

The First 60 Minutes of Your Day

Prepare for the day ahead.

Use your first 60 minutes to review your diary for the day, block out meeting times and a lunch break (yes, you do need to eat and take a break away from your desk, if only for a few minutes). Now look at how much time is left to 'do work' and schedule tasks realistically. Most people's 'to do' lists end up being impossibly long – we're not likely to get through them in a month, let alone by the end of the day, so it's important to prioritise your tasks. Ask yourself, 'If I could only accomplish three things today, which would deliver the best results?' These are your 'A' priorities and where you need to focus your efforts. Allocate the remaining items on your list 'B' or 'C' ratings: the 'B's can wait until they become 'A's another day, and ask yourself whether the 'C's really need to be done at all? Your day may not end up looking as chaotic and jam-packed as you're used to, but you will find that you achieve more and are more in-control of your time – and the bonus is, you'll feel better and produce a better quality of work.

Book a meeting with yourself.

Treat your first 60 minutes as a standing appointment with yourself and protect it from being eaten into by other people's meeting requests. Over time, people will learn that you are not available and they'll work around you.

Tell everyone.

It is important to let your team know what you're doing and why, so they'll learn to understand and respect your quiet time and work around it. Encourage others to also use the first 60 minutes practice – with the benefit of time for planning and thinking everyone's results will improve.

Ignore the ringing in your ears!

Switch your mobile phone off or to silent mode and set your desk phone to voicemail. We have become far too contactable, between telephones, mobiles, SMS, voicemail and email it is possible to spend your entire day responding to other people. Be sure to develop good practices for replying and over time people will learn that you are not always available but they'll trust you to get back to them.

Hang a 'Do Not Disturb' sign.

If you have an actual office with a door, this one is easy, but many workplaces today are open plan and it's difficult to alert people to the fact that you don't wish to be interrupted. I know one workplace where each person has an item (in this case, a toy frog) which when placed on top of their computer means that they are not available. When the frog comes down, everyone knows that they are available again. With the agreement of everyone in the team this system works well in an open plan environment. Another technique is to use headphones, when people see that you have headphones on they know you are not tuned-in to what's happening around you. You don't even have to be listening to anything if you find that too distracting, just put your headphones on to signal your 'do not disturb' request.

The Last Ten Minutes Of Your Day

Quitting time.

Just like your first 60 minutes, you need to block out the last ten minutes of your day to make time for your end-of-day routine.

Look ahead.

Start your 'to do' list for the next day while your focus is still on the job – it's far more difficult to do in the morning when you're wondering where you left-off the day before. Carry over any incomplete tasks from your current day's list and add new priorities. It helps to clear your head to put all this on paper and you'll be amazed at how much more effective you can be when your brain power is being put to problem-solving rather than trying to remember everything you need to do!

What's in store?

Check your diary and commitments for the following day and be aware of what's coming up, where you need to be and what preparation, tasks and projects you need to focus on.

Leave it clean.

Clear and tidy your desk, throw rubbish in the bin, sort leftover mail and papers and put your files away. Clean your coffee cup, empty your water bottle, wash any leftover dishes or containers from lunch and start each day afresh. By clearing your workspace you also signal the end of the workday to your mind.

Carry your reading.

If you don't already have one, start a reading file and carry it with you on your way home. You can get through a surprising amount of reading on public transport to and from work.

Shut down.

Switch your phone to voicemail, remembering to change your message if you're not going to be in the next day, or if you're going to be in late. Close out your email, and activate your 'out of office' message if you're going to be away, switch off your computer, screen and printer.

Making Time Work for You

Time is one of our most rare and valuable resources and in today's generally over-worked and under-resourced workplaces we must learn how to spend it wisely. To boost your productivity you must constantly ask yourself, 'How can I get the best return for my time?' And remember that once it's spent – you can never get it back again.

Book it in.

Block out regular meetings and activities in advance, including work, family and social commitments. Schedule these in your diary as soon as they arise and for as long as they will continue – this way you won't forget important appointments or double-book yourself. Using colour coding can help you to distinguish between work, family and fun activities at a glance.

Make time for the regulars.

Schedule time for regular activities such as the first 60 and last ten minutes of your day, weekly reports, project updates and monthly newsletters. You know these activities will come around, so don't leave them until the last minute or over-book yourself with so many other meetings and activities that you can't find time for them.

Make time for a break.

Block out your holidays and short breaks at the beginning of each year. By scheduling and planning your holidays in advance you'll not only have something to look forward to but you'll have a much better chance of avoiding the usual pre-holiday stress that comes from trying to complete everything before you go. Letting your colleagues and clients know in advance when you've scheduled your holidays for also means that everyone can plan for your time away. It is also good practice to block out time for lunch every day. Too many people work through the day without even a 15 or 20-minute break away from their desks in the sunshine and fresh air. Human beings are incapable of working at full capacity for such extended periods of time, so schedule a break every day and take it.

Remember travel time.

So many people only schedule time for the meetings they attend and forget to plan the time needed to travel to and from the venue. Book in travel time whenever you make an appointment and be sure to allow yourself a buffer in case of bad traffic or other delays. Travel time can be put to good use returning calls, thinking about and planning projects, listening to motivational or educational CDs or even just enjoying some relaxing down-time. And, before you do travel, ask yourself whether it is really necessary – could you save time by teleconferencing instead?

Before and after.

The other thing most people overlook is the need to schedule time before and after each meeting to prepare and complete follow-up activities. We're so used to rushing from meetings straight back to our desks, only to immediately get caught up in returning calls and responding to emails and colleagues, that the work that comes out of meetings doesn't get done until long after. Scheduling time will allow you to turn up prepared and to action minutes, follow-up on projects and complete tasks that arise out of the meeting while the information is still fresh in your mind.

Protect your time.

It's especially important to block out time for all of your activities and commitments if other people have access to your diary. Only allow access to those people who have a real need to book time with you and give them clear guidelines about the meeting bookings you will accept to prevent them from wasting your time. If you have a personal assistant, make sure that he or she understands which appointments can be made without your approval and which must be referred to you first. This will ensure you are only seeing people who have a direct impact on your results.

Keep a backup.

If you've ever lost your diary or data you'll know that it can virtually bring you to a standstill, as well as cause embarrassment and hassle when you can't remember which appointments you had when. Keep a backup of your diary. If you use a paper diary photocopy it weekly, if you use an electronic diary synchronise it with your computer and back it up weekly.

Desktop Management

Many of us spend long hours at our desks, so to help make the workday more comfortable and productive it helps to create an environment conducive to clear thinking. By establishing a good desk environment you are guaranteed to improve your efficiency and achieve more in your day.

The paperless desk.

Remove all paperwork from your desk – create files for your projects, reference folders for information you need to access regularly, a reading file for articles, reports, journals and FYI documents and a daily file for administrative, miscellaneous and day-specific tasks. Keep your files on shelves or in drawers. The only thing on your desk at any point in time should be information relating to the task or project you are currently working on.

Out of sight, out of mind.

Remove your in-tray from your desk or get rid of it altogether if you can! Keeping it out of sight helps to prevent you from getting distracted by the growing pile of things you need to do and stops people from dropping things in it without you noticing.

Avoid double-handling.

Many people believe that you should only handle paper once. This may not always be practical, however if you get into the habit of making 'action notes' either directly onto, or attached to, each piece of paper it will remind you of what you need to do with each item when it comes back to the top of your list.

Stationery drawer.

Keep stationery in cupboards or drawers rather than on your desk. Get rid of all the clutter and keep your desk clear for essential items relating to the current piece of work you are doing.

Set up a comfort zone.

Take the time to set up your PC, monitor, phone, chair and other vital tools properly. Make sure they are within easy reach and are positioned for comfortable use.

Inspire yourself.

Surround yourself with positive images. Keep a photo or phrase that motivates you in view to remind you of and motivate you toward continually striving for your goals.

File It

Despite the best of intentions, most of us don't use good information management practices, the mountain of paperwork piles up on top of us like an avalanche, and beyond that there are PC files, emails and SMS messages to organise too. Organising, sorting and systemising information is not something that most of us have ever been taught how to do – so it's hardly surprising that we struggle to find order among the chaos. Effective information management is essential to your efficiency and productivity, introducing simple systems and investing just 15 minutes per week can put you back in control of your information.

Managing Paperwork

Keeping it together.

Create a central storage area for everything that requires filing – a box or a folder labeled 'filing' – and throw everything into it during the week.

Make time.

Allocate 15 minutes per week to filing. Depending on the state you are in at the beginning, you may need to allocate more time than this to get on top of the task, but from then on 15 minutes per week should be a small enough time slot to find, but long enough to keep you on top of your paperwork.

Set up systems.

When using filing cabinets, decide how you will allocate your space to make it easiest to locate your files. For example, rather than mixing all your files together you might decide to keep current customer files in one drawer and potential customer files and marketing information in another drawer, or you might choose to store current projects in one drawer and research and reference information in another – you get the idea – look at the type of files you have and decide how to logically divide them into categories.

Colour it.

Use colour coding to further systemise your files as well as to enable you to identify different types of files at a glance. Choose a range of coloured manila folders and allocate a different colour to different file types, for example, blue for customer files, purple for staff files, pink for project files and so on. Make a reference list of what each colour represents until you are familiar with your new system.

What colour is today?

Now set up a different coloured folder for each day of the week. Use these to file tasks that require action on certain days. Check the contents of your daily files as part of your ten-minute preparation at the end of each day and prioritise the tasks. Make sure you keep your day files up-to-date by immediately filing papers relating to your daily tasks in the appropriate day file.

Managing Email

Virtual files.

Set up folders in your email to file important information that you have read or actioned and want to keep for future reference. These folders might mirror your hardcopy files to make it easy for you to cross-reference printed and online information.

Online colour.

Learn how to colour code your incoming email so that you can identify at a glance which emails require your immediate attention. Again, your colour coding might mirror your hard copy filing system as well as include some new colour categories for emails from friends and family.

Email rules.

Establish rules for incoming email to help you sort the legitimate messages from the spam, jokes and junk. Your email software can help you to send spam messages directly to your trash, or to send e-zines or newsletters that you subscribe to directly to a reading folder.

Read and delete.

Many people have a tendency to want to keep emails – set yourself some guidelines for what you want to keep and delete the rest once you have read or actioned them. And, don't keep emails in your inbox – they'll only make you feel like you have more work than you really do and increase the chances you'll overlook something that needs your attention. Be disciplined – read, action and then file or delete.

Spring clean.

Schedule time to clean out your email regularly, once a month should be enough to keep on top of it. Empty your deleted items and any unnecessary sent items, and go through completed project or task folders to clean out anything that is not essential for your records.

Effective Phoning

One of the things that most impacts people's productivity is not being able to focus on completing one task at a time and telephone calls, both making and receiving them, are one of the greatest disruptions to the flow of the day and to our ability to concentrate. By managing how and when we make and receive calls we can not only make better use of our time but make a better impression on the person at the other end of the line, too.

Incoming Calls

Don't pick up.

The phone is a tool for your convenience – use and respond to it when it suits you. Some people can't ignore a ringing phone, try thinking of the phone as a question, when it's ringing someone is asking you if you are available to speak and it's your choice whether it suits you to speak now or to let the call go through to voicemail and respond later. You'll be more productive because you won't be breaking your train of thought every time the phone rings, and it's more considerate to your caller. We've all had the experience when someone who is clearly busy, distracted, frustrated or in a rush answers our call – it puts both people in an uncomfortable position and it would have been fairer for them to allow us to leave a message and to respond at a more convenient time.

Introduce yourself.

Answer the call by introducing yourself clearly, 'Good morning, Neen James Communications, this is Neen James speaking,' this identifies you and your business to your caller.

Pay attention.

If you do decide to answer the call do your caller the courtesy of paying attention. Disinterest or lack of attention can very easily be heard in your voice – as can the typing that you continue to do while making all the right 'aha' sounds. Stop what you are doing and pay attention, or tell the caller you'll call back later if it's not a convenient time.

Relax.

Speak as though the caller is sitting across the table from you and use your usual face-to-face conversational style, rather than a special 'telephone voice'.

Smile.

It is a proven fact that a smile can be 'heard' on the other end of the phone. Your callers will appreciate your friendly approach.

Stand up.

If it's an important call or one you are nervous about, stand up. When you do, it allows more air to circulate through your lungs, your voice will sound more relaxed and maintain an even tone which can also give you an 'air of authority'.

Keep it short.

You'd be surprised how much time is wasted on the phone. There's nothing wrong with politely managing the conversation so that it gets straight to the point, for example, 'Hi Dave, what can I do for you today?'

Thanks for calling.

Always end by thanking your caller for calling.

Outgoing Calls

Make a time.

Allocate a specific time to make your outgoing calls, including return calls to people that have left messages for you. This way you won't disrupt yourself mid-task to make a call you just remembered you need to make. You'll also be better able to focus on the conversation and the needs of the person you are calling when you are focused on the call, rather than trying to fit it in while you're concentrating on something else.

Think before you speak.

Think about the call before you make it – know the reasons why you are calling and what you want to come out of the conversation. Also, think about the timing from the point of view of the person you are calling – consider whether you are calling them at a time when you know they'll be trying to get out the door, or when they're likely to be busiest in their own business, and schedule your calls for appropriate times.

Clear your desk.

Clear everything from your desk that does not relate to the person you are calling to avoid becoming distracted or tempted to try and do two things at once. Make sure you have any previous correspondence or materials that you'll need to refer to on hand.

Identify yourself.

Unless you are absolutely certain that the person answering your call will know who you are and where you are from, identify yourself clearly at the beginning of the conversation. If you are contacting someone for the first time it can be useful to give them a context – it will save both of you any embarrassment and allow the person you are calling to focus on what it is you are saying, rather than wondering who you are, for example, 'Good morning Simone, this is Neen James from Neen James Communications calling; you might recall we met at Jennifer's book launch last week?'

When you say 'this is' before stating your name it alerts your caller that you are about to say your name, which makes it easier for them to take note, especially if they don't know you. Make sure you enunciate clearly – there's nothing worse than when someone speaks too quickly or mumbles and you have to ask again, 'Sorry, who's speaking?'

Is this a good time?

Another essential phone call opener is to enquire as to whether you are calling at a convenient time. Many people will answer the phone at even the most inconvenient times, which usually results in them feeling annoyed at you! So ask: 'Good morning Simone, this is Neen James from Neen James Communications calling; you might recall we met at Jennifer's book launch last week? I thought I'd give you a call to discuss that project we were talking about – is now a convenient time for you?'

Leave a detailed message.

If you don't get through to the person you are calling, leave a detailed message – whether by voicemail or with the person that does answer the phone. Make sure you include the time and date that you called, a brief mention of what you are calling about and how and when they can contact you. If you are going to be difficult to catch or have scheduled some time during which you won't be taking phone calls yourself, by leaving a contact time you can avoid a frustrating game of 'phone tag'.

Mobile Calls

Leave a message.

Provide message bank for your callers. There's nothing more frustrating than trying to contact someone that does not have the courtesy to provide the facility to leave a message when they are unavailable. In your recorded message let callers know when they can expect to hear from you, for example, 'Please leave a message and I will return your call within 24 hours'. Tailor your messages according to your schedule and if you are travelling or on holidays, let your callers know when you will be returning.

If you call a mobile phone that is diverted to message bank – leave a message. The person you are trying to reach may only be available to check their messages and return calls at a certain time, if you don't leave a message they won't be able to call or SMS you and you'll become frustrated at not being able to contact them.

Clear your messages.

Clear your message bank regularly and make return calls or send SMSs to people who have left messages for you within an appropriate period of time.

'Turn if off.'

There must be a lot of people that don't realise that mobile phones have 'off' buttons! Switching off your mobile at certain times is a demonstration of courtesy and respect for the people you are with or the place you are in. In meetings and seminars, at meals, in church, at the theatre, movies or other public places – turn it off. Your callers will be able to leave you a message and you can return the call at a more appropriate time.

Do it in the lift.

Get into the habit of turning your phone to silent mode or switching it off in the lift on your way to meetings, and switching it back on to check your messages in the lift on the way out of meetings. This simple ritual will save you the embarrassment of your phone ringing during an important meeting. If you are expecting a call that you absolutely must take, explain that you are waiting for the call and may need to be excused when it comes through. Switch your phone to silent and discretely exit the room to take the call when it comes.

Keep it short.

Many people are uncomfortable with lengthy mobile phone conversations for a number of reasons – health, privacy and cost among them – so keep it short and to the point.

Can you talk right now?

If you are making the call, acknowledge that the person you are calling could be with other people, on the bus, train or driving, or somewhere where they can't hear you properly or speak loudly – always ask, 'Can you talk right now?' before launching into your conversation.

Consider the time.

Be considerate about time and, unless there is good reason, don't contact people on their mobile number outside of business hours.

Who else is there?

If you answer a call while you're in your car, let the caller know you're driving. If you are on speakerphone and there's a passenger with you, let your caller know who's with you to avoid any embarrassing situations and to ensure confidentiality.

First things first.

Always be professional and considerate. If you decide to take calls when you are with other people, excuse yourself and leave the room but remember the people you are with may feel less important than your caller. Use message bank, silent mode or just switch it off until you are available again.

Hang up and lock up.

We've all heard horror stories of mobile phones not properly hung up or keypads not locked and the last number called being accidentally dialled so that the person inadvertently called is privy to your conversation without you being aware that they are on the line. Ensure that your phone is hung up properly and use the keypad lock facility to avoid potential disasters!

Email Etiquette

You may remember a time before there was email…a time when communications within most organisations were more formal and followed strict lines of protocol. Email has done wonders to break down some of the communication bureaucracy and hierarchy within organisations; today virtually anyone can speak to anyone else within an organisation with the click of a mouse – which can have both exciting and devastating implications! Email has brought with it a new informality to business communications – but it didn't come with instructions. Over time, a generally unspoken email code of communication has emerged. Master email etiquette, and you'll not only be on safe ground but people will enjoy reading and responding to your emails.

Your signature.

Use your email program to create an email signature block that will automatically attach to all of your outgoing messages; it's a little like an email letterhead. It saves you the effort of including your contact information every time you send a message and brings a professional touch to your communications. You might simply include your name, business name, contact details and website or you might also include a sentence or two about your business, a special promotion you are running with a link to your website, or even a favourite funny or inspirational quote.

We're all different.

Take care when creating email signatures and stationery to keep it simple – just because it looks good on your computer doesn't mean it'll arrive in that same format at the other end. The way your stationery will display is dependent on the email software of your receiver – what is a smart-looking email design on your screen could easily turn out looking like an incomprehensible mess at the receiving end.

Think sharp.

Because email is a screen-based communication, we must write for the screen, not the page; think and write in bullet points. Keep your sentences short and to the point. Longer content might be best captured as an attachment that can be printed out and read.

Size matters.

Be considerate when sending emails with attachments, especially to people outside of your organisation; not everyone will have the same file size limits and fast access that you might have and a large attachment can potentially block your receiver's email account for many minutes.

Watch your tone.

Business communications used to all share a fairly dull, formal tone of voice and an official looking layout. Email is much more informal, and allows for a casual and personal approach – but this can lead to misinterpretations – people can misread your tone of voice, especially if they don't know you. There are ways to lessen the chances of inadvertently causing offence, such as: not writing complete words or sentences in capital letters (in e-speak capital letters indicate shouting); always using a greeting ('Hi', 'Hello', 'Good morning' and 'Good afternoon' are probably more common and appropriate than 'Dear'), and using emotion icons such as :o) or :o(can be friendly and help clarify your tone or mood.

Spelll chceck.

Email makes each one of us an instant author and that's not necessarily a good thing! Always, always re-read your emails before you send them to make sure they make sense and to fix any spelling or grammatical errors. I recommend you set your email to automatically spell-check every message before it is sent. And if you need a second opinion to check for clarity, tone or correctness, ask a colleague to look over the content for you. It might be inconsequential to you, but a poorly worded email that conveys the wrong tone and is riddled with spelling and grammatical errors can destroy your credibility.

Reply quickly.

Because of its immediacy, people expect fast replies to emails. A response within 24 hours is probably as long as most people would consider appropriate. Your email practices will educate others about what to expect from you in email communications; if you respond quickly, people will expect that you'll always respond quickly; if you set a 24-hour benchmark, likewise people will learn what to expect from you – but of course there will always be those emails that do require your immediate attention. Whatever you choose as an appropriate email turnaround, let people know what to expect, and be consistent.

Schedule email time.

Email messages popping into your inbox all day long can be an enormous distraction, particularly if your email is set to alert you every time new mail arrives. To check in on your emails and respond to them as they arrive not only distracts you from whatever tasks or projects you are working on but can rob you of an entire day responding to other people's needs while your own are neglected. Schedule a few times each day to check and respond to emails rather than constantly looking-in on your inbox or being bounced there by your email program with every new message.

Out of office.

Use your email 'Out of Office' facility if you are going to be unable to respond to emails within your usual timeframe – this might be because you are away or you might choose to use the 'Out of Office' reply to buy you some quiet time while still managing other people's expectations about when they can expect to hear from you.

Use your BCC.

In your email address block, apart from the 'To' field, there are generally two others, 'CC' (courtesy copy) and 'BCC' (blind courtesy copy) which we can use to send an email to someone without the other recipients knowing. If you are sending a bulk email, put the addresses of all of your recipients in the BCC field; it protects their privacy by not disclosing their names or addresses to each other as well as making your email communications 'neater' – each recipient does not receive a lengthy list of all other recipients' details.

Who needs to know?

Email makes it so easy to include as many people as needed in a communication. The downside is that some people stop thinking about who needs to know what and just copy everyone in. Think about who needs to action your email and who really needs to read and be aware of it and only include those people in the recipient list. If you do have multiple people on an email distribution, let each person know what is required of them and by when.

Use with caution.

The ease and immediacy of email make it a communication tool to use with caution. The wrong email sent to the wrong person or people can have devastating implications. I know of someone who was fired after inadvertently sending the wrong email to a list of people and in doing so transmitted confidential information, which was not only damaging to the individuals, but also exposed the organisation to legal action for breach of privacy; I know of others who have embarrassed themselves and others by mis-sending gossipy emails; and I know some friendships that have ended up on the rocks because of the wrong email being sent to the wrong person. Be careful about how you use email – once you click that 'send' button, it's gone.

Working Well With Others

Many office environments these days are open plan, with only a few senior managers having offices of their own. This style of work can have great benefits for team building, fostering cooperation and collaboration, and can be wonderful for developing the social aspects of teams, but on the flipside, it can drive some people crazy and reduce productivity. Open plan offices require people to learn how to work together in very close proximity, which can present challenges, particularly relating to how we manage the physical environment, the noise and the constant interruptions. Share some of these strategies with your team to help you to achieve a working environment where everyone is respectful of the needs and space occupied by others.

Keep it down!
It's easy to overlook how far your conversation can travel in a confined space – be aware of what you can hear of others' conversations and remember that they can hear yours too. Especially if you are loud or have a unique voice (like me!), be aware of your volume.

Walk the floor.
Don't yell across workstations, walk over to the person's desk or use your email or phone, not everyone in the vicinity needs to be disrupted by your conversation.

Be careful where you stand.
Don't stop for conversations or hold impromptu meetings at other people's workstations – be considerate. If you want to have a meeting, choose a space that won't impact others.

Get a room.
If there are two or more people and you don't have a discrete area to meet, book a meeting room and be sure to tidy it up before you leave.

Anyone for music?
If you like listening to music, keep it down to a level where it doesn't interfere with the concentration or comfort of your colleagues. If everyone agrees, you might choose a particular style of music and play it at an appropriate volume. Otherwise, buy yourself some headphones and keep the music to yourself.

Telephone etiquette.
Be considerate about how you manage your phones, the constant ringing of desk phones and mobiles with their various show tunes and other 'ditties' can be distracting and annoying. Turn your ringer-volume down rather than let it blare throughout the office and try to answer your phone or have your voicemail pick it

up within three rings. If you will be away from your desk for a prolonged period divert your phone to your mobile or voicemail.

Take a message.

Answer your neighbour's phone if it is appropriate to do so. If you take a message send the details to them in an email immediately to avoid lost phone messages on scraps of paper.

Hang a 'Do Not Disturb' sign.

I've mentioned this one before, but it's worth repeating here. Agree among your team on a signal that will indicate that you are unavailable – that you are trying to concentrate on something or are on a deadline and do not wish to be disturbed. It might be an item placed on top of your computer monitor or desk, or even a sign taped to the back of your chair. When the signal is up, everyone agrees not to disturb you, when the signal comes down, people know that it's business as usual again.

Clear desk policy.

Adopt a clear desk policy, it makes the overall environment more pleasant and comfortable (rather than looking like a hurricane has been through) and it's excellent for both personal productivity and security.

Stash it away.

If you need some extra storage space, make use of the area under your desk, but be careful not to crowd yourself.

Smile.

Include some personal touches on your workstation, but don't overdo it – you and your workstation are on display to your team and others who pass by your area, and you want to give a professional impression. Choose a photo of your family, a picture of a place you dream of going to or something else that inspires you and makes you feel happy.

Learning to Share

Too often we convince ourselves that we can, or should, do everything. We say things like 'it would be quicker to do it myself' or 'no one else would do it as well as I do' and we convince ourselves that we are irreplaceable. Working to become an indispensable asset to your team is an excellent goal but knowing where to focus your efforts and when to share the load is even more important. Failure to delegate appropriately reduces your productivity and prevents you from achieving your goals. Choose to become more productive by delegating to others – you'll give them the satisfaction of learning something new, reward them with more responsibility, free up your own headspace to focus on other things and empower everyone to achieve more.

Give it up.

Recognise and admit to yourself that you can't do everything all of the time. Let go of needing to be in complete control. Acknowledge that you will benefit from other people's help and give them the opportunity to shine in the process. Learn to become comfortable with delegating. You don't need to delegate responsibility if you choose not to, but you can at least delegate tasks and functions to others.

Trust yourself.

You already believe you are the best person to do the job – now believe that you are the best person to delegate tasks to others. Trust in your ability to teach and give other people the best instructions on how to complete tasks.

Trust other people.

One of the biggest reasons people don't delegate is because they don't trust other people to complete a task or activity in the same way as they would themselves. And this is absolutely true: no one will do things exactly like you. Accept that something done by someone else 80 per cent to your liking may be better than having to do 100 per cent of it yourself. Accept that maybe your way is not the best way and that someone else might even do better than you. Either of these results is good – everyone benefits. Try delegating small tasks at first to build trust in yourself and your delegate.

Create a process.

Establish a template for task delegation. Write down specific details of the action and timeframe required along with references to any documentation or key stakeholders involved. Work through this sheet with the person you are delegating the task to. This helps you to both be clear on what is being asked and what resources are available or need to be considered.

Clear timeframes.

Often when delegating we get frustrated because people don't complete things in the same amount of time as we would. Be specific about the date and time you want the task or activity completed, and tell people why so that they understand why your deadline is so important. Also, understand that while people are learning something new, it may take them a little longer.

What do you expect?

Communicate your expectations clearly and specifically – people don't read minds! Make it very clear if there is a particular way that a task must be completed.

What was that?

Ask your delegate to summarise, in their own words, their understanding of the task – what is expected, by when and how it is to be completed. At this point you can answer any questions and clarify any misunderstandings.

Feedback.

When complete, let the person know how they performed according to your instructions, expectations and timeframes. Recognise their achievement through praise or an appropriate reward.

Congratulations!

Congratulate yourself for trusting someone else to complete activities or tasks that you would normally do yourself.

managing your
position

Making an Impression

Did you know that you have just seven seconds to make a first impression? In little more than the blink of an eye everyone you meet will make a judgement about your age, income, marital status, education, interests and more. They may or may not be right about you, only time will tell. On any given day you never know whom you might meet and how making the right impression on the right person could set your career or life on a new path. Take steps to make sure that you make a memorable impression (for all the right reasons) on the people you meet...and who knows where that'll lead to?

Appear confident.

There's an element of 'fake it til you make it' here. Smile when you first meet someone and look him or her in the eye. Even if you don't feel it, your smile and eye contact will show the other person that you are friendly and confident.

Be aware of your body language.

Be aware of good posture; stand up straight with your shoulders back. Don't fidget with pens or your clothing – if you are a 'fidgeter' focus on keeping your hands comfortably by your sides.

Introduce yourself first.

Rather than standing alone, be brave. Walk up to someone or a group of people, extend your hand and say, 'Hi my name is Neen James, nice to meet you'. You'll find that people will respond positively to your confidence and appreciate you making the first move – and it'll be a trigger for others to do the same.

Shake hands.

If you don't know how to shake hands properly, learn, it is an important skill and a big part of creating a first impression. Cultivate a firm handshake not too hard, but just right. Look the person in the eye when you shake their hand and say their name out loud: 'Hi Robyn, it's nice to meet you'. If you are unsure about whether or not to shake hands, avoid that awkward moment by taking the initiative and extending your hand first. And remember, it is extremely rude to not shake the hand of someone who offers theirs to you.

Learn how to pronounce their name.

When you meet someone with a difficult to pronounce name, ask him or her to repeat it, spell it and say it again and allow him or her to correct your pronunciation so you get it right. People will appreciate you taking the time to learn how to say their name properly.

Say it again.

Use a person's name several times when you first meet. This will help you to remember their name and it's a very personal way to communicate – people love the sound of their own name!

Learn conversational skills.

The ability to make conversation is what scares so many people about new business and social interactions, here are a few questions you can ask anyone you meet for the first time:

- What do you do?
- Where do you work?
- Where do you live?
- Does it take you long to get from home to the office?
- What inspires you?
- What do you like to read?
- What has been your most valuable business lesson?

Also ask people what they like to do in their spare time. This is a great question and most people become energised when you ask them about their life outside of work; watch their eyes sparkle as they tell you about the activities they most enjoy.

If you meet someone with an accent, ask where he or she is from and find out something interesting about their country by asking:

- Where are you from?
- How often do you go back to visit?
- What do you miss most about that place?
- Who is someone famous from there?
- What food is that country famous for?

If you are at an industry or charity event, ask how they heard about the event. It's a great icebreaker and allows you both to share stories about how you came to be at the event and what you hope to achieve by attending.

Listen intently.

Give the person you are speaking with your full attention. Use active listening techniques such as nodding, smiling, leaning toward them and asking questions about the things you are discussing. People will appreciate your attention. It is very rude to look beyond the person you are speaking with or around the room for someone more interesting.

Networking

While there is any number of different networking groups and events that you can attend, some of the best networking can happen within your own organisation. Boosting your profile by being involved in both professional and social events can substantially improve your opportunities when it comes time for promotion or appointment to special projects. Building strong relationships with key people throughout your organisation can also help you to access information, gain support for initiatives, influence decision makers and tap into other people's internal networks and spheres of influence. It is well worth investing time in. Try some of these networking activities to boost your profile.

Professional Networking Activities

Hold a 'brown bag' seminar.

Identify a topic that you and your colleagues are interested in (it might be work-related or something of general interest such as health, fitness, work/life balance, financial planning) and invite everyone to bring their lunch along to a lunchtime seminar. The presenter could be either internal or external to your organisation, the important thing is that he or she is an expert on the topic. Set the agenda so that there is time for people to meet and chat when they arrive, allow 20 minutes for the presentation, ten minutes for questions and a few minutes at the end for conversations and mingling. Make a point of taking the opportunity to meet someone from another department each time you hold a seminar.

Invite your CEO to breakfast.

Invite your CEO to attend a quarterly breakfast where he or she can meet with your team for an informal question and answer session. Book the meeting dates in everyone's diary well in advance and make sure that people commit to attending. Ensure that you start and finish on time so that the breakfast doesn't interfere with anyone's other commitments for the day.

Mix it up.

Invite another team to morning tea where team members can get to know each other and talk about what they do within the organisation and the challenges that they face. This is a great way to learn more about others and how different parts of the company work together, as well as to share information about the projects each team is working on.

Join a team.

Seek out opportunities to work on projects both within your team and with other departments. This is a great way to demonstrate your abilities and to build relationships as well as to learn from others.

Offer to be the MC.

If your organisation is having a conference or event, offer your services as the master (or mistress) of ceremonies. You'll not only have the opportunity to meet and work with people throughout your organisation but also with any external consultants that might be involved.

Become a correspondent.

Offer to provide articles or updates for the internal newsletter. This is a great way to position yourself as someone who knows what's going on and to get your name in front of the whole organisation.

Leave your card.

When you meet someone from another department always offer them your business card. If you work in a very large or widely dispersed organisation this will help them to know how to get in touch with you again.

Seek out (or start) a mentor program.

When you invest your time in being a mentee you are rewarded with accelerated learning and experiences from your mentor. If your organisation offers a mentoring program, sign up and get involved. If there isn't a formal mentoring program, suggest one or identify people that you would like to learn from and approach them about mentoring you. If you do approach someone about being your mentor make sure you present yourself professionally and show your prospective mentor that you are serious and committed by having a mentoring plan in place.

Social Networking Activities

Join the social committee.

Every business has a social committee whether formal or informal. Invest some time in volunteering for the committee and helping to organise fun activities through which you and your co-workers can get to know each other. Plan for a variety of social events that give everyone the opportunity to get involved and to occasionally include their families.

Get involved in a charity.

Identify a charity or good cause and invite someone from the organisation you choose to support to provide regular updates on their activities and suggestions about how people can get involved. This can be a fun way to help others while helping you get to know the people you work with.

Start a club.

Find people who are interested in similar books to you and start a book club. When you get together, talk about what you learnt from the book, your opinions on the writing style and what you liked most about it. If the author is local, invite him or her to join your meeting.

Go for drinks.

Suggest that your team finishes at 5pm on Friday afternoons and meets at a local bar or café and invite other teams to join you. Make the 'official' time for drinks between 5pm and 6pm so that those who want to get away feel comfortable doing so.

Organise a lunchtime sports team.

This is a great way to build teamwork and get to know people from other areas within your organisation. Put up a notice or send an email asking for interested parties and form a basketball, football, tennis or soccer team or even a walking club. Meet at a nearby oval, park or gym at the same time each week. This is a great way to get some fresh air and exercise while networking.

Happy Hour

No, this isn't about Friday night drinks – it's a different type of Happy Hour, one designed to keep your staff happy and your team morale and relationships on track. A Happy Hour is a regular one-hour appointment that you make with each of your team members individually. It is one-hour of your undivided attention where each team member sets his or her own agenda. It could happen weekly, fortnightly, monthly – whatever is most appropriate for your team and workplace – and it can happen either face-to-face or via teleconference if you are in different locations. Happy Hour gives each team member time with you to use as they see fit, to discuss their own individual needs, issues, objectives and development. You'll be amazed at how your team's performance improves with just one regular hour of one-on-one time with you.

Get everyone on board.

Make sure that everyone understands the benefits of Happy Hour – it can boost morale, build relationships, help to improve individual and team performance, help to balance team personalities and address issues before they become problems. As a manager, it gives you the opportunity to maintain regular contact with each member of your team and to have a good insight into how the whole team is performing.

Be clear on what it's not.

Part of the success of Happy Hour is in making sure that everyone understands that it is not an excuse to duck out for a drink with the boss or to complain about other team members. Happy Hour should be solely about focusing on improving performance, discussing objectives and building results.

Be consistent.

Allocate a regular time for each Happy Hour appointment, whether it is weekly, fortnightly or monthly. Schedule this time in everyone's diaries well in advance. This will help to ensure that your Happy Hour meetings happen consistently and it gives your team members a certain time each week, fortnight or month when they know that they'll have time with you to raise issues. This will translate into fewer ad hoc meetings and interruptions because people will save any non-urgent issues for their Happy Hour appointment.

Keep to time.

As with all meetings it is important to keep strictly to your allocated time. This not only ensures that you and your team members can keep all your other commitments, but also helps your team to learn how to manage their hour with you effectively and prevents any office politics resulting from you spending more time with one person than others.

Be prepared.

Help your team members to learn how to put together appropriate agendas for their Happy Hour with you. Remember, this is their hour and they are setting the agenda – this is not a time for you to delegate work to them or to run your own agenda.

Get away.

Allow each team member to choose his or her preferred location for their meeting. Make sure they choose somewhere that you will both be uninterrupted and be open to leaving the office to sit in a nearby café if that is their preference; this can make for a more relaxed meeting and it gives you the opportunity to interact with each other outside of the office environment.

Switch off.

Make sure you both switch off your mobile phones for the duration of the meeting.

Be honest.

Happy Hour is an opportunity for open and honest conversations and feedback. It is up to you to make sure that your team members feel like they can discuss issues with you openly. Make a commitment to helping them by being open and honest in your feedback and advice to them.

Measure it.

Happy Hour meetings should be accountable. Check that all agenda items have been addressed, issues resolved or actions identified before you close the meeting.

Great Team Work

If you want to achieve amazing things, surround yourself with a great team. Even if you are in business on your own, you can still build a team of suppliers that can help you to achieve your goals. Stop trying to do everything yourself and find great people to help you. High achievers know that their team is one of their most valuable assets, keep them motivated and the sky is the limit!

Ask.

Find out what motivates each member of your team. Not everyone is motivated by the same things – make a note so that when you want to recognise an individual for his or her performance you'll know how to do it best. How do you find out what motivates someone? It's simple, just ask.

Keep them in the loop.

Keep your team up-to-date with company information, new clients, performance against targets, customer complaints, compliments and competitor information. Always ensure that they are aware of both the positive and negative aspects of your business.

Communicate.

The best way to keep your team motivated is to create an environment in which people feel important, valued and trusted. Do this by speaking with your team every day, walking the floor and being seen, having regular team meetings and reviews.

Give negative feedback quickly.

If you have a concern or issue with one of your team, address it immediately. Make a time to have a chat, explain what the problem is and ask them how you can solve it together. Don't let negative emotions or situations build up to the point where they become bigger than they should. Get onto it quickly.

Share talents.

Allow people within your team to learn about each other's roles. This way when someone takes time off, you know your business is covered. It also keeps people learning and interested.

Have a back up.

If you run a virtual team (where you are not all located in the same place), source multiple suppliers for vital components of your business. This ensures that your business will flow, even when some of your team are not available.

Get together.

Hold team meetings every week. It might not be possible to get the whole team together every week so meet with the people who are available and make a special effort to get the whole team together at least once per month. Regular team meetings build relationships, improve communication and help to fuel creativity.

Inspire them.

Expose your team to high achievers, people you admire. Bring people into your office to 'tell their story' about how they achieved success and to answer questions from your team members. You could source these people from your own network, your mentors or contact your local Speakers Bureau.

Support a charity together.

Identify a charity that best represents your company and values and spend time as a group fundraising or attending events for this great purpose. This is a great common goal for any team and creates excellent team spirit.

Give away a charity day.

Allow each of your team one day per year to support their chosen charity. Don't take this from their annual leave, give them a bonus day to support their community.

Increase responsibility.

When people perform well, reward them by increasing their responsibility and autonomy. When the opportunity arises, give people the chance to step into more senior positions to cover for colleagues who are away and give them the opportunity to learn new tasks and develop their skills.

Educate them.

Provide opportunities both internally and externally for your team to expand their skills. This might include holding in-house training, paying for people to attend courses and programs run by external organisations or developing an on-the-job training program.

Review.

Make time every six months to meet with each team member individually to review his or her progress against targets. Once every year, set aside time to review their progress and document their achievements, areas for development, new performance targets and provide an overall summary of their results.

Surprise!

Do something occasionally that makes each person feel valued as a member of the team. This might include putting on a special morning tea for everyone, paying for pizza and drinks for lunch, leaving a chocolate or flower on each person's desk, writing a handwritten thank you note or organising a guest speaker/celebrity for your next team meeting.

Praise.

Make trying to catch people doing something right a part of your daily routine, and make sure you always praise people for doing the right thing.

Just rewards.

Use incentives, rewards and recognition to acknowledge a job well done. This might include extra time off, movie tickets, bonus money, more responsibility, a bottle of wine or acknowledgement at the next team meeting.

Coaches and Mentors

A career coach or mentor is a person who can guide you with the benefit of their experience. He or she may be someone more senior from within your organisation or someone external to your organisation who has been successful in the field you are interested in. The right mentor can help you accelerate your career, boost your self-development and improve your working relationships. And remember that a mentor is not only helpful in your career, the benefits of having a mentor are relevant to all areas of your life – whether it's fitness, finances or lifestyle.

How can they help you?

Take an objective look at which areas of your life you'd like guidance with. When you know which areas you want to focus on you can begin searching for a suitable mentor.

Who are the top performers?

Whichever area of your life you decide to seek a mentor for, find out who the experts are, who does it better than anyone else? Next, find out where your role models hang out – check out networking events and groups, industry events and conferences and take note of anyone who stands out and has the 'presence' you are looking for.

Look into programs.

Many organisations offer internal mentoring programs. If you work for yourself you can investigate government departments that offer mentoring programs.

Select your mentor.

When you identify the person you believe would be a suitable mentor, spend some time watching them in action. Ask around to find out what other people's opinion of your chosen mentor are and find out all you can about their achievements, beliefs, values and way of operating. This will give you an insight into them before you approach them about mentoring you.

Approach your mentor.

Phone your prospective mentor and ask for an appointment to meet with them. It is important that your interactions are professional and show respect for your prospective mentor's time.

Have an agenda.

When you do meet, have an outline of what you would like to discuss. Your agenda should include why you want them to mentor you, for how long and what you hope to gain during that time. If they do agree to mentor you, you can then work out how you can support them too – this should be a two-way process.

Make an agreement.

If you both decide to proceed, set up an agreement and guidelines about how your relationship will work and what you expect from each other.

Coaching and Counselling

If you manage other people, from time to time it will be a necessary part of your role to provide feedback and guidance to someone who is not performing at their best. This can be challenging and confronting – for both you and your team member – especially when you have a great working relationship because it can be difficult to step into the role of 'manager' without risking the status quo. But with a little planning and a few winning techniques you'll both be more comfortable and more likely to have a true win-win interaction.

What's the process?

Most organisations have human resources policies that describe the way any formal counselling session must be managed, begin by finding out what these are. If your organisation doesn't have a policy, seek advice from your human resources or other senior manager. You may need to seek advice outside of your organisation if there aren't appropriately qualified people internally. For a range of reasons, including legally, you must ensure that you undertake this process within the bounds of your organisation's policies and the applicable laws.

Get coaching or training.

If you are uncertain about the best way to conduct the session, seek advice. Your manager or human resources manager will be able to assist you. Ask for help with the structure and content of the session – it's a good opportunity to share your perspective and ideas with someone.

Choose your location.

Where you choose to hold the session is important and will give your staff member clues as to how serious the issue is and perhaps how supportive you are. A meeting held in the boardroom sends a different signal to one held in your office or at a quiet coffee shop. Select a location that offers privacy and that says something about the intention of the meeting.

Advise your team member.

Alert your team member to the general content of the meeting beforehand, don't ambush him or her. Give a few days notice so that he or she also has time to prepare, but not so long that they become stressed and distracted. Make sure that others in the team are not aware of the issue or the purpose of the meeting.
If the issue is serious and you intend to conduct a formal counselling session, advise your team member that he or she may have another person accompany them as a witness if they believe it is necessary. You might also choose to invite the human resources or another manager to witness the meeting if you feel it is appropriate.

Be prepared.

Record the meeting in your calendar as a counselling session and make a note on the team member's staff file. Set an agenda for the meeting and give it to your team member in advance.

Use appropriate language.

Be sensitive to the situation and aware that your team member may be feeling upset, stressed or angry, it is up to you to manage the meeting professionally. Be factual and give specific examples of situations you have been unsatisfied with. Tell your team member specifically what you expect and give him or her the opportunity to share their side of the story. Avoid generalisations and stick to the facts. Avoid becoming defensive, aggressive, raising your voice, swearing, blaming or using unnecessary descriptions.

Practice active listening.

Make sure that you are in an environment where you can't be easily distracted, switch off your mobile phone and ensure you will be otherwise uninterrupted. Maintain eye contact, focus on the person you are speaking with and take accurate notes to serve as a record of the meeting and its outcomes.

Mind your body language.

Be conscious of the way you sit – avoid defensive body language, such as folding your arms and leaning too far away from the person, and aggressive body language such as pointing and leaning too far forward. If possible, sit beside the person you are counselling rather than across the table from them.

Take note.

Always take detailed notes of the time, date and who was present at the meeting. Write down any actions that are agreed and repeat them back to your team member to make sure everything discussed is clear to both parties. You might decide to have both your team member and yourself sign a written record of the meeting and its outcomes to ensure that everyone is in agreement.

managing yourself

Make This Your Best Year Ever!

Make an appointment with yourself for the first of January every year to reflect on the year that was, and the year yet to come. By following these simple steps, you'll start every year on the right foot and make sure that each one is better than the last.

No more New Year's Resolutions!

Focus on creating realistic goals for all areas of your life – health, career, finance, personal development, relationships and giving. Write each of your goals down and choose to make this the year that you achieve them. Put your goals somewhere you will see them every day.

Go for health.

Your health can be either your greatest asset or your greatest liability. Too many of us only think about our health when it's at risk. Make investing in your health a top priority. Schedule a check-up with your doctor, take a close look at your diet and choose to make daily exercise an absolute must. Protect your health as you would a rare and precious treasure.

Use it or lose it!

I recently read that people who spend a thousand dollars or more each year on their personal development will increase their business by 20 per cent. Read more books, attend workshops, find a new networking group, listen to tapes or CDs in your car, do online courses or enrol in college or university. Keep your brain active.

Make time.

Eliminate time-robbers from your day – make a list of all the things you do that rob you of your time, such as watching too much television, running errands inefficiently, checking and responding to your email too often, making long phone calls, waiting in traffic and even spending time with other people. Focus on controlling your time, organising your day efficiently and getting rid of the things in your life that are not a high priority.

VIPs only.

Surround yourself with VIPs (very inspiring people) and eliminate VDPs (very draining people). Spending more time with VIPs will inspire, motivate and invigorate you. Minimise the amount of time you give to the VDPs in your life. It can be difficult to make the switch – but be strict with yourself and you'll reap the rewards of being among the VIP crowd.

Where are you going next?

Plan your next holiday, even if you're already on one! Allocate time in your calendar and start collecting brochures – it'll give you something wonderful to look forward to and ensure that your holiday has top priority before your diary starts filling-up for the year.

Love those that love you.

Balancing work and home is a challenge, and often it is those closest to us who miss out on the best of us. Choose to be more focused on those you love and don't forget to remind them how much they mean to you. Promise yourself that you won't take anyone for granted this year. I try to tell one person every day that they are special to me – maybe you could try this too?

Give it attitude.

We're all familiar with setting daily 'things to do' lists – I also create a daily 'attitude to do' list. My list includes things like tell someone they are special, send a thank you note, sit in the sun for 15 minutes, find something funny, choose to be positive and exercise. What will your list include?

Choose to be amazing!

It's as simple as making a commitment to yourself every morning that you will have an amazing day. Remember, life is not a dress rehearsal – we only get one performance, so let's give it our best!

Go Confidently

Of course we are more productive when we feel good about ourselves and our abilities, when we feel like we know exactly what needs to be done and how to make it happen…but we don't always wake up feeling that way. Even people who look like they have never had a crisis of confidence in their lives, have. The difference is that they have effective strategies to get back on top on those low confidence days, or at the very least, they know how to fake it! It's up to you to be your own biggest fan; when you believe in your own capabilities others will too. Easier said than done? Try these strategies to help restore your confidence in yourself.

What are you good at?

Identify and know what it is that you are good at, now is not the time for false modesty or bravado – be realistic. Reflect on your achievements to date and write a list of the things you are very good at – all of your talents, skills and competencies – and refer to it whenever you need to remind yourself that you are valuable.

Stop the chatter.

Tell that little voice in your head to stop putting you down! How can you possibly hope to feel confident when there's someone inside your head telling you that you 'can't do it', 'aren't good enough', 'aren't smart enough, pretty enough, skinny enough, experienced enough…' all day long? Catch yourself whenever you are being negative in your self-talk and change it to positive.

Like yourself.

Write down what you do and don't like about yourself. Embrace those things that you do like and make plans to improve those things that you don't – it's time to stop beating yourself up and do something about them. Know that you are unique – there is no one else on this planet with the same qualities, experiences, ideas and gifts as you.

Trust yourself.

Look for examples of times in your life when you have made good decisions and trust yourself to be able to do it again. If you take the time to identify and know the beliefs and values that guide you, you can trust that your internal 'radar' will point you in the right direction.

Create a confidence journal.

Write down how you feel each day for 30 days in a confidence journal. This will help you to track your responses to different situations and to identify habits and circumstances that shake your confidence. When you understand more about how you feel and respond to different situations, you can develop strategies to help you overcome those challenges in the future.

List your 'energy toppers'.

Make a list of all the things you love to do and keep it somewhere handy to refer to on those days when you don't feel 100 per cent. You might list simple things that recharge you such as going for a bushwalk or watching the sunrise. My friend Robyn Henderson begins her day at 5am walking on the beach and photographing the sunrise every morning, what a beautiful way to start each day.

Know your 'energy zappers'.

Be aware of those tasks and activities that you don't like and the people that drain your energy. Make a conscious decision to limit the amount of time you spend doing those things or with those people. If it is possible to avoid them altogether for the sake of your wellbeing, then do so.

Choose to Be Happy!

We've all heard the saying, 'Life is not a dress rehearsal', but we often spend our time as though it were. We each have 86,400 seconds per day and we can choose to spend them feeling happy, depressed or miserable. Happy people are more energetic and productive. But happiness doesn't always come naturally. Feeling happy is something that we all have to work at from time to time. Every day I make a new choice to be happy and you can too with the help of these happiness strategies.

Play music.

It's difficult to feel unhappy when you're listening to uplifting music. Find a copy of Jimmy Durante's 'You gotta start off each day with a smile' – it's guaranteed to help you do just that!

Laugh out loud.

Many people get into the habit of suppressing their laughter, not wanting to draw attention to themselves, particularly if they have a loud or unique laugh. Stop suppressing your laughter make it loud and long and don't worry about who hears you. Laughter is contagious, so if people do hear you, you'll be giving them a giggle too.

Play with kids.

Playing with kids can be great food for the soul – just being in their world for a while will bring you joy. If you don't have your own kids, play with someone else's.

Cuddle a pet.

Pets, like kids, are great for the spirit – they find joy in simple things, give unconditional love and will always come back for more affection.

Help someone.

When you are feeling down or sorry for yourself one of the best things you can do is help someone else. It might be a friend, colleague or family member, or you could do something good for someone you don't know through community or volunteer work. Taking the focus off yourself and giving your time and attention to someone else can be incredibly rewarding and renewing.

Reflect on flowers.
Buy yourself some flowers and enjoy their beauty and complexity. My favourites are pink starburst lilies, they have a wonderful fragrance and last for a week. I buy them regularly for my home and office.

Light a candle.
A plain or fragrant candle is quieting, relaxing and rejuvenating. Look for candles with aromatherapy oils and benefit from their restorative properties too.

Learn to meditate.
Get into the habit of meditating, spending a few quiet minutes with yourself every day. This can be wonderfully rejuvenating and you can do it just about anywhere. Meditating can help you to replace negative thoughts with calm, peaceful thoughts.

Buy a giggle.
There are plenty of ways you can buy yourself a giggle. I used to keep a laughter bag on my desk – when you squeeze it, it giggles. The giggles are contagious and it was worth every cent. Why not go to a comedy show at your local comedy club or hire a funny DVD, someone like Billy Connolly or Bill Cosby, these are oldies but goodies that are certain to make your sides split with laughter.

Kicking Goals

There's a lot written about goal-setting and there are many different approaches and methods – in fact, it's easy to get so caught up in the confusion about how to set goals properly that you don't end up setting any. These simple steps will help you to set powerful goals and make goal-setting an invaluable part of your life. You'll be amazed at what you can achieve with the help of some well thought-out written goals – try it!

Make a date.

Make time in your diary and find a quiet, comfortable location to set your goals. Every January I spend a morning at my favourite table in the tearoom of the Sheraton on the Park (a beautiful hotel in Sydney) to review my goals for the year that's just finished and to set new ones for the year ahead.

Take five.

Create five categories for which to set goals: physical, educational, spiritual, financial, and relationships. By setting goals for each of these areas you will be sure not to neglect any important aspects of your life.

Write it.

You must write your goals down – it makes them more powerful. Use positive language – words like 'I will' and 'I am' – this will help you to feel as though you have already achieved your goals and to change your behaviours accordingly, for example, 'I am going to the gym three times per week'. Make sure you allocate a specific timeframe for the completion of each goal, for example, 'By the beginning of March, I am going to the gym three times per week'. Now, identify a reward for achieving each goal. This will inspire you even more toward the achievement of your goal. And finally, list the possible obstacles that could get in the way of you achieving each goal, and how you will overcome them. This will help you to pre-empt the things that might go wrong so that if they do you can immediately swing into action with your solution, rather than giving up on your goal.

Share.

Make yourself accountable to someone you trust. Share your goals with them and ask them to check in with you regularly to make sure you are on track.

Review constantly.

I have been told that the difference between a millionaire and a billionaire is that a billionaire reads their goals twice a day, and a millionaire only once. I keep a copy of my goals in several places around my house (on the bathroom mirror, on the printer in my office, outside the shower screen, on the fridge, on my bedside table and in my wallet), which makes it easy for me to see my goals and be reminded of what I am working toward several times a day.

Keep track.

When you return to your favourite place next year, review your progress and take time to feel proud of the things you have achieved before you move on to setting goals for the next year.

Healthy, Wealthy and Wise

We all strive for a 'balanced life', and although we may not be able to achieve that elusive state of balance all of the time, we can certainly be moving in the right direction by focusing on these three key areas. By managing our health, growing our wealth and seeking to improve our knowledge and understanding in all that we do, we can become more productive and achieve amazing things.

Get checked.

Make an annual appointment with your healthcare practitioners for a check-up. In less than a couple of hours per year, you can ensure that your body is functioning well and get advice on any niggling health issues before they turn into big health issues. Go to the dentist, get your eyes checked, have any spots on your skin monitored and talk to your doctor about the specific health checks you should be having depending on your age and whether you are a woman or man. Don't put this one off – make that appointment this week.

Eat well.

We all know what we should be eating and drinking more of and less of, yet in the daily rush we eat on the run, consume way too much take-away food and don't slow down to really enjoy the pleasure of preparing and sharing meals with our loved ones. Learn more about nutrition and enjoy the unique pleasure and feeling of wellbeing that comes from really eating well and taking care of yourself.

Get comfortable with yourself.

Women in particular will relate to the seemingly constant challenge of trying to feel comfortable with our bodies. We only get one body – and we have to live with it for a lifetime. We can choose to make a commitment to helping it work as well as possible – or, we can spend a lifetime disliking it and feeling upset that it isn't the one that we wanted. What do you think about your body? Do you stand in front of the mirror despising parts of it, or are you proud of your curves, muscles and physique? You can choose to celebrate your body or to condemn it, but remember you only have one, so why not choose to marvel at what a miracle it is and make the most of the body you have.

Daily exercise.

Schedule at least four or five exercise sessions each week, so even if you miss one, you'll still have plenty of opportunities. These days the good news from the experts is that all we need to do is 30 minutes of moderate intensity exercise on most days of the week to get real benefits, and that's not too difficult to fit into your schedule. Make exercise fun and interesting by including a variety of activities, such as walking, boxing, running, yoga, weight lifting, Pilates or martial arts. Recruit an exercise buddy and make exercising a great opportunity to catch up with each other. And don't forget that incidental exercise can be just as effective as other workouts – so take the stairs, get off the bus a couple of stops early, park your car at the far end of the car park and take every opportunity to get up and move, even if it doesn't seem like much, every little bit really does count.

Early to bed, early to rise.

Sleep is vital for renewing body and mind and yet we often forfeit sleep time so that we can do other activities. Get into the habit of going to bed and waking up at the same time each day and unless you have a good reason (such as if you are a shift-worker) try to make sure you're in bed by 11pm and up by 7.30am – adjust the times to suit you, depending on whether you are a morning or evening person and what your schedule allows. The important thing is to discipline yourself to get a good night's sleep and rise early so that you can make the most of every day.

Unplug.

Schedule at least one television-free night each week. Switch off the set and instead listen to your favourite music, play a board or card game, read a book, enjoy a quiet meal by candle light (alone or with someone whose company you love), go on a date or soak in a bath. Start being aware of your television viewing habits and make a point of only watching programs that you truly enjoy and stop wasting precious time in front of the television.

Switch it off.

Protect your time (and your sanity!) by switching off your mobile phone and setting your landline to voicemail when you are trying to complete an important task or enjoy a relaxing activity. Change your message (if it makes you feel better) to let people know when you will be available again and when they can expect to hear back from you.

Get your house in order.

You will feel more in control of your life when your home is a retreat rather than an obstacle course or a constant reminder of things that need doing! Spend some time spring-cleaning – remove the clutter, tidy problem areas, create storage solutions and eliminate the mess. It could take you weeks, but the results will be worth it, and once your house is in order make a commitment to keeping it that way.

Read well.

Reading is a wonderful pastime, it can transport you to incredible places – both real and imagined – as well as improve your mind, memory and conversational skills. Make a commitment to reading widely and look for a variety of books, both fiction and non-fiction, that interest you. There's usually plenty of down-time in most people's days which is ideal for reading, such as on public transport, on your lunch break and before bed. If you're not a keen reader, try listening to audio books on cassette or CD instead.

Keep learning.

It really is true that if you don't use it, you lose it! Keep your mind active and interested by enrolling in a part-time course at your local college or community centre. You could choose to do something to help your career or something just for fun and interest. There is an enormous variety of courses offered in most areas, everything from learning a language to updating your IT skills, sushi making, scuba diving, presentation skills, car maintenance and so much more.

Save money.

Getting your finances in order is a great stress-saver. It can be confronting to get real about your financial situation, but until you do there's no hope of getting your finances under control. Seek help if you need to from a financial planner or even a friend, colleague or relative who knows what they're doing. It's a wonderful feeling knowing that your spending is under control, that you have money in the bank and that you can pay all of your bills. Start by keeping track of where you spend your money for a month (every single cent) and review it at the end of the month to see where your money really goes. Like most people, you'll probably find that there are plenty of ways you can save, such as eating at home more often, taking your lunch to work and avoiding impulsive purchases.

You are What You Eat

To boost your energy you need to supply your body with good quality fuel, but when we get busy our diet is often one of the first things that we let go. You cannot fuel your body with caffeine, sugar and take-away food and expect to be functioning at your best either physically or mentally. These days, there's no shortage of books, magazines, websites and healthcare professionals that can help us to create a high-fuel diet and there are even companies that will deliver pre-packaged, nutritionally balanced meals direct to our front doors. So the only other challenge is to make eating well an important part of your daily routine. Try these simple strategies to incorporate good food habits into your life and you'll reap the rewards by looking better, feeling better and performing better.

Make time.

How often do we end up either eating something fast and fattening or nothing at all simply because we don't have time? Book some non-negotiable time in your diary for lunch every day, no matter how busy you are. You will be far more productive in the afternoon if you make time for a lunch break. Get out of your work or home environment, go for a walk or sit in a park and enjoy your lunch. If you don't have an hour, make it half an hour or even just 15 minutes – the mental break, the physical movement and the nutritious food will restore you.

Eat with others.

Plan to use your mealtimes to catch up with friends, family and colleagues. By using mealtimes as productive social and business opportunities, you'll be less likely to eat poorly or to skip meals altogether.

Create a plan.

Being organised is one of the great keys to success in all things, and it's no different where your diet is concerned. Create a list of meals in advance and stick it to your fridge so that you know what meals you are going to have during the week (and you'll avoid those dreaded 'What are we going to have for dinner?' conversations!). By doing this you can plan your shopping in advance and always have an interesting and nutritious meal on the table.

Share it.

Make meal preparation a social part of your day – recruit your partner, flatmates or family to help you prepare meals – while their talents may vary, everyone is capable of pitching in. This not only relieves one person from having responsibility for all of the meals, but it can also be a wonderful time to catch up on the day and enjoy each other's company. If you live by yourself, share the cooking with a friend, when you cook prepare enough for two and swap meals with each other.

Create an atmosphere.

Encourage your partner, flatmates or family to sit and eat together. Set the table, put some music on and light a candle to create a relaxing atmosphere. Too often we eat separately or are so distracted by the television that we miss out on the opportunity to spend quality time together. You are also more likely to eat faster with the television on, and sometimes we can be so distracted that our brains don't even register the fact that we've eaten at all, and that's when we overeat. If someone is insistent on watching the news or a favourite program, change the mealtime to a time when everyone can be completely present.

Try new foods and flavours.

Keep your taste buds tantalised with a variety of foods. Try new, exotic fruits or international flavourings to keep your diet varied and interesting.

Shopping list.

Shop monthly for pantry items – things in cans or packets that have a long shelf life it'll save you time and if you stock up when they're on special, you'll save money too. Shop throughout the week for fresh foods such as bread, fruit, vegetables and so on. Online shopping can save you time and money and most stores will deliver right to your kitchen so you can place your order online anytime that suits you and have your groceries delivered – it doesn't get any better than that.

Move It!

We all know that regular exercise benefits both body and mind; a fit, strong body and sharp focused mind are two of the most valuable tools you can have, but it can be a real struggle to get there. For many years I'd set myself the same New Year's Resolutions to get fit, go to the gym and lose weight. And usually, two weeks into January I'd have blown my resolutions and feel guilty for 'not achieving my goals'. Then, coming from a place of guilt, disappointment and even defeat I would be less able to make the positive changes that I needed in my life. Sound familiar? What I discovered was that it is more important to make movement a part of my every day routine (notice that I used the word 'movement', not exercise!). Making small changes can help you to make exercise part of your life, rather than something that you 'have to do' – try it and enjoy the benefits!

Make an appointment.

Start with three 30-minute exercise sessions per week and schedule the time in your diary well in advance. One of the main reasons that people don't exercise is because they think they don't have time so book it in and make time. Choose whatever time of day best suits you and your schedule; for some people that will be the early morning (and it's a wonderful feeling knowing that you've exercised before breakfast and don't have to think about it for the rest of the day!), and for others it will be during the day, at lunchtime or after work.

Recruit a buddy.

Find someone you can be accountable to – they don't necessarily need to exercise with you (but it can be more fun with someone else) as long as you are accountable for reporting your exercise activities to him or her. You might even have a variety of exercise buddies, one for walking, one for the gym, one for tennis – whatever works for you. I have a great gym buddy, Simone, we have a laugh, work hard and keep each other inspired.

Distract yourself!

Combine your daily exercise with other activities to make great use of your time and keep yourself interested. Try setting up your home gym near your TV and watch the news while you workout, or get out your headphones and listen to music or a motivational audio book.

Join a gym.

If you enjoy group exercise, or simply like having access to great equipment and organised activities, join a gym. Make sure you choose a reputable company, that it's close to your home or work (if it's not convenient you won't use it), that the classes you're interested in are on at times that suit you and that there is plenty of staff available to help you. If you've never joined a gym before, don't be intimidated. Most gyms these days offer many forms of exercise (apart from weight lifting and high-impact 80s-style aerobics!), including yoga, tai chi, cycle and even walking and in-line skating groups – there really is something to suit everyone.

Keep it fresh.

Another thing that stops people from exercising is boredom, so keep your exercise choices fresh, rather than just doing the same thing day-in, day-out. On weekends, grab a ball and head to the park, buy a basketball and play one-on-one with your partner or flatmate, drive to the nearest beach, park or lake and go for a long walk, try skating, do a gym class that you've never tried before, buy a yoga DVD, join a soccer club, start a dance class, get some kids (or adults) together and play tag and other childhood games – the options are endless, just keep moving and having fun!

Get a personal trainer.

If you are having trouble getting motivated on your own (or even with a gym buddy), or if you'd just like someone to help you establish an exercise program, think about investing in a personal trainer – they're no longer just for the rich and super fit. A personal trainer can help you to kick-start your fitness plan and be a great source of encouragement and accountability. When choosing a trainer make sure they are appropriately qualified, that you like him or her and that you trust them to help you achieve your goals. If they are more interested in talking on their mobile phone or staring at themselves in the mirror while they are training you, find someone new. Many gyms have personal trainers on staff and there are also independent trainers who operate out of either their own fitness studios or public gyms. You can also find trainers who won't take you anywhere near a gym if you're not interested in that type of activity – there are plenty of other ways to get fit!

On a budget?

You don't need a lot of money to exercise just invest in a good pair of walking shoes and you're ready to go. Walking is one of the best forms of exercise and it's available to everyone regardless of how old you are, what size you are or how much money you have.

Set goals.

Keep a list of things you want to achieve through your exercise, it might include physical challenges such as running up the stairs without getting puffed, walking 4km in less than an hour or completing a full gym class without stopping, as well as health and self-esteem goals such as losing weight, improving your cardiovascular fitness, fitting into your summer clothes with confidence and so on. Write your goals down and read them every day to remind yourself of the wonderful achievements you are striving for.

Keep track.

Encourage yourself by keeping an exercise journal. Record your training sessions and any new milestones you achieve. For example, when you first begin exercising you might have poor flexibility and after doing yoga classes and stretching you find you can reach your toes! Keep track, it's fantastic to have a record of all your hard work and to see how far you've progressed.

Reward yourself.

Find ways that are meaningful to you to reward yourself for all of your hard work and dedication – but preferably not with chocolate! Buy yourself a new pair of walking shoes or gym outfit, have a massage or a soak in the tub with candles, music, sweet-smelling oils – the works!

Sleep Tight

Do you often wake up after a night's sleep feeling like you've only been asleep for a few minutes? Or can you take a 'power nap' and feel like you've been asleep for hours? Can you sleep anywhere or do you need your own pillow for a good night's sleep? We all have different relationships with sleep, some of us can sleep easily while for others it's a struggle every night. Sleep is so important to our health, and it can affect our productivity greatly, so we must ensure that we get enough quality sleep to keep our bodies and minds functioning at their best. For most of us, all it requires is a little planning...

Create an environment conducive to sleep.

A comfortable bed is key to having a good night's sleep; invest in the best quality bed, pillow and linen that you can afford and ensure that your blankets or doonas are of an appropriate weight for your body temperature. If you sleep with someone else, you might need to consider each having your own special blankets or doonas, especially if you have different (and incompatible) night time body temperatures.

Get ready for bed.

Develop a pre-sleep routine that you follow every night. Having a night time ritual signals to your mind that it is time to quieten down, which in turn prompts your brain to send the appropriate sleep signals to your body. Remember, it takes 21 days to form a habit so stick with it until your pre-sleep ritual becomes routine.

Have a bath.

Relaxing in a warm, scented bath is a wonderful way to unwind and help your body and mind prepare for sleep. Try a few drops of pure lavender or chamomile essential oil, or experiment with other relaxing oils and blends in your bathwater.

Take a deep breath.

Take three deep breaths; deep breathing can help you to relax and prepare your mind for sleep. Try also taking a very deep breath, holding it for a couple of seconds and then blowing it out hard – this is like getting rid of the rubbish from the day – three of these will ensure that you get rid of any negative thoughts or feelings leftover from the day.

Take a note.

If you are someone who lies awake thinking over problems, the next day's tasks or making plans, place a notepad and pen beside your bed. When you find yourself lying awake troubling over an issue or with your mind racing, write down some notes or reminders to yourself and put it out of your mind until the morning.

Read a little.

Reading can be another wonderful way to quieten body and mind and prepare for sleep. Shut yourself away from any background noise, dim the lights and read a few pages. Try not to read anything too riveting or anything work-related…this is time to relax. As soon as you feel your eyelids dropping, put down the book and drift off to sleep – don't fight the urge to sleep just so you can finish the page – you might miss the 'sleep wave' and end up staying awake for hours!

Arrange your room.

If you can, allow fresh air to circulate through the room while you sleep. Block out the light with blinds or heavy curtains and remove televisions, computers, telephones, mobile phones and other electronic equipment from the room or at least move them away from the head of your bed. Not only can these prove distracting, but there have been studies that have shown that the waves and frequencies emitted by electronics can interfere with a sound night's sleep.

Go natural.

Try sleeping in the nude – it's liberating and with no clothing to get bunched up, wrapped around you or to overheat you, you may find that you sleep better.

Money Management

As someone who loves to shop, enjoys holidays and owns way too many pairs of shoes, managing my finances is definitely something that does not come naturally to me, I have had to learn. Managing your money is so important in becoming more organised, less stressed and more productive in your life – you'll be amazed at what you can achieve with your money when it starts working for you, rather than you always working for it!

Seek advice.

It's funny how most of us will go to experts for help in so many different areas of our lives, but we seem to think that managing our money is something we can handle ourselves – usually when all evidence is to the contrary! Look for a financial planner or accountant that can help you set a course for your financial future – they can help you to identify your financial goals, get real about your budget and set up investment strategies – you'll wonder why you didn't do it sooner.

Budget is not a dirty word!

I know for many people 'budget' and 'diet' are in the same category, but a realistic budget is a phenomenally powerful financial tool and is imperative if you want to take control of your money. Budgets can, and should, leave room for money to have fun with and to reward yourself with for all of your savings efforts! If you find establishing a budget difficult to do (or to get motivated to do) on your own, seek help from a financial professional or even a friend, colleague or family member who has it all together financially.

Keep track.

Keep a written record of every cent you spend for 30 days to see where your money is really going. This activity serves a number of purposes – firstly it probably shocks you into reality and secondly, it helps you to identify categories of spending which you'll need to include in your budget. Remember, keep track of every single cent…at the end of the month if you're spending more than you're earning that'll be a good indication of where some of your financial stress may be coming from!

The big picture.

As well as looking at your day-to-day spending, estimate your annual expenses by looking at all of your regular bills and financial commitments and totalling that amount for the whole year. Once you know what your total fixed liabilities are for the year, divide that amount by 12 for a monthly figure. This is the amount you should be putting away each month just to pay your bills.

Keep on top of it.

Review your budget weekly – this is a great habit to get into and helps you to keep on top of where your money is going and to quickly identify areas where you are spending too much – it can be quite an eye-opener! You might create a spreadsheet to enter your income and expenses into and to keep as an ongoing record.

Credit or charge?

Swap your credit cards for charge cards that you pay off in full each month. Knowing that you have to pay it off at the end of the month is a great motivator to help you get past those impulse purchases. If you do want or need a credit card, keep your credit limit low to help stop you from spending too much.

Go online.

Bank fees and charges are one of those small expenses that don't seem like much each time, but they can add up. You can easily avoid them by changing your banking habits. Online banking is ideal; it's cheap, convenient, reliable, saves you time and helps you to understand your financial position 24-hours-a-day.

Keep your receipts.

How many times have you wished that you kept the receipt – whether it's so you can return or exchange an item or claim it on your tax? Set up a simple receipt filing system – it doesn't have to be complicated, an alphabetical file will do, and you'll be able to find anything you need without the stress.

Tax time.

Keep a separate file for your tax receipts and other documents relating to your annual tax return. This will save you from the frustrations at the end of the financial year and help you (or your accountant) to make sure you maximise your chances of receiving a tax return.

additional reading
& resources

Behind every super productive person there is a secret list of resources – the books they read and the websites they love – here is my list. I have put this together for you so you can instantly access the resources and books that will help boost your productivity in each of the four main areas of your life. All you need to do is find the area you want to work on and check out the additional resources that will help you in that area. Read the books, review the websites, subscribe to newsletters and magazines – these are my hand-picked favourites.

Managing your career

Books

Body Language: How to Read Other's Thoughts by Their Gestures, by Allan Pease. Australia: Camel Publishing Company, 1987.

Fish: A Remarkable Way to Boost Morale and Improve Results, by Stephen C Lundin, Harry Paul and John Christensen. London: Hodder and Stroughton, 2000.

Good Better Best: A Guide to Developing and Managing Your Profile, by Victoria L Hansen. North Sydney: Hi Profile Management, 1992.

How to Win Friends and Influence People, by Dale Carnegie. New York: Simon & Schuster, 1981.

Oh, The Places You Will Go! By Dr. Suess. New York: Random House, 1990.

Reach for the Stars, by Janet Terban Morris. New York: Peter Pauper Press Inc, 2002.

The Little Book of Calm, by Paul Wilson. Australia: Penguin Books, 1996.

Websites

Barbara Woodward Enterprises – exceptional resources for career transitioning and outplacement services. She also offers the services of a resume coach – www.bwepl.com

Officeworks – great range of stationery for all occasions – www.officeworks.com.au

Staples – great US company for stationery supplies – www.staples.com

Tymson Communications – learn all the secrets behind gender communications with legendary business educator and keynote speaker, Candy Tymson – www.tymson.com.au

Services

Image Consultant – the very talented, Megan Kristel – www.kristelclosets.com

Ink Communications – editing services are essential for resumes, proposals and any communications where you want to make an impact! Ask for Simone Tregeagle – www.inkcommunications.com.au

Networks

LinkedIn – great tool for managing an electronic network – www.linkedin.com

Network Central. This fantastic network is designed to create communities for busy business people – www.networkcentral.com.au

Women's Network Australia – one of the best women's networks I have ever seen. Lynette Palmen has created an awesome resource for women all over Australia – www.womensnetwork.com.au

eWomen Network – Exeptional network for women supporting other women in business – www.ewomennetwork.com

CD Packs

How to Achieve Amazing Things in Your Work Life, by Neen James. Sydney: Neen James Communications, 2004. On CD 1 find more tips on how to ask your boss for a pay rise – www.neenjames.com/products

Managing Your Work

Books

The 7 Habits of Highly Effective People, by Stephen R Covey. New York: Fireside, 1989.

25 Dumb E-Mail Mistakes That Internet Users Make ... and how to avoid them, by Gihan Perera. www.firststep.com.au

Don't Sweat the Small Stuff... and It's All Small Stuff: Simple Ways to Keep the Little Things from Taking Over Your Life, by Richard Carlson. New York: Hyperion, 1997.

Empowerment Takes More Than a Minute by Ken Blanchard and John P Carlos and Alan Randolph. San Francisco: Berrett-Koehler Publishers Inc, 1996.

First Things First, by Stephen Covey, A. Roger Merrill, and Rebecca R. Merrill. New York: Fireside, 1995.

Getting Things Done: The Art of Stress-Free Productivity, by David Allen. New York: Viking, 2000.

More Hours in My Day, by Emilie Barnes. Oregon: Harvest House, 1994.

Saving Time: Really Simple Solutions for Really Busy People, by Lynee Wenig. Melbourne: Anne O'Donovan, 1999.

Simply Organized, by Emilie Barnes. Oregon: Harvest House, 1997.

Storage, by Sibella Court and Karen McCartney. Sydney: Murdoch Books, 2000.

The Greatest Salesman in the World, by Og Mandino. New York: Bantam Books, 1968.

The Personal Efficiency Program: How to Get Organised and Do More Work in Less Time, by Kerry Gleeson. New Jersey: John Wiley & Sons. Inc, 2004.

The Procrastinator's Handbook: Mastering the Art of Doing It Now, by Rita Emmett. New York: Walker Publishing, 2000.

Women Who Do Too Much: How to Stop Doing It All & Start Enjoying Your Life, by Patricia H Sprinkle. Michigan: Zondervan Publishing House, 1992.

You Don't Have to Be Born Brilliant: How to Design a Magnificent Life, by John McGrath. Australia: Hodder, 2001.

You Inc., by John McGrath. Sydney: Harper Collins, 2003.

Websites

Email Power Tip of the Week, by Gihan Perera. This delivers a powerful tip for using email more effectively once a week – www.firststep.com.au

Getting a Grip on Time series by Robyn Pearce – www.gettingagripontime.com

CD Packs

Get More Done. How to become massively productive and get on with it – CD pack by Matt Church and Neen James. Sydney: Matt Church Pty Ltd, 2004 – www.neenjames.com

Managing Your Position

Books

Be Seen, Get Known, Move Ahead: A Beginners Guide to Self Promotion, by Robyn Henderson and Marg McAlister. Coogee: Networking to Win, 1998.

Business Etiquette: 101 Ways to Conduct Business with Charm and Savvy, by Ann Marie Sabath. New Jersey: Career Press, 1998.

Masters of Networking: Building relationships for your pocketbook and soul, by Ivan R Misner and Don Morgan. Atlanta: Bard Press, 2000. This international resource features Robyn Henderson, Global Networking Specialist.

Network or Perish: Learn the secrets of master networkers, by Robyn Henderson, Belinda Yabsley, Neen James, Kim McGuinness, Jennifer Jefferies, Lee-Anne Carson, Sue Henry and Sandy Forster. Kingscliff: Sea Change Publishing, 2004.

Networking Magic: 366 Hot Networking Tips, by Robyn Henderson. Coogee: Networking to Win, 1999.

Purple Cow: Transform Your Business by Being Remarkable, by Seth Godin. New York: Penguin Group, 2002.

The Coach, by Ric Charlesworth. Australia: Pan Macmillan Australia Pty Limited, 2001.

Upfront & In Control, by Peter Miller & Ron Tacchi – www.achieving.com.au

Websites

Australian Thought Leaders – www.australianthoughtleaders.com – if you are an infopreneur, this site is for you.

David Price – the 'Meetings Guru' – www.davidprice.com – learn all the meeting tips from the master.

Networks

Connect – Marketing Professionals Network. Great network designed for marketing and communications professionals. Contact Carolyn Stafford – www.connectnetwork.com.au

CD Packs

How to Achieve Amazing Things in Your Work, by Neen James. Sydney: Neen James Communications, 2004. CD 2 details how to be a mentee, how to find a mentor and how to be a mentor – www.neenjames.com

How to Run a Successful Home Based Business, by Robyn Henderson & Neen James. Kingscliff: Sea Change Publishing, 2004 – www.neenjames.com

Information Empire, by Robyn Henderson. Sydney: Networking to Win, 2002. – www.networkingtowin.com.au

Managing Yourself

Books

7 Steps to Sanity, by Jennifer Jefferies. Gold Coast: Living Energy Publishing, 2005. www.jenniferjefferies.com.

Awaken the Giant Within. How to Take Immediate Control of Your Mental, Emotional, Physical & Financial Destiny, by Anthony Robbins. New York: Simon & Schuster, 1992.

Big Bucks, How to make serious money for both you and your company, by Ken Blanchard and Sheldon Bowles. Great Britain: HarperCollins Business, 2000.

Body for Life: 12 weeks to mental and spiritual strength, by Bill Phillips. New York: Harper Collins, 1999.

Chicken Soup for the Soul, by Mark Victor Hansen and Jack Canfield. Deerfield Beach: Health Communications, 1993. These excellent books are full of stories that will warm your soul.

Happiness Is, by Lisa Messenger. Sydney: Messenger Publishing, 2004. This colourful book is full of pictures of Aussies doing what makes them happy (and I'm on page 117) – www.happinessis.com.au

How to Stop Worrying and Start Living, by Dale Carnegie. New York: Simon & Schuster, 1984.

High Life 24/7: Balance Your Body Chemistry and Feel Uplifted, by Matt Church. Sydney: ABC Books, 2002.

Laughter, Sex, Vegetables and Fish: *How to Survive and Thrive Under Stress*, by John Tickell. Melbourne: Bookman Press, 1995.

Liver Cleansing Diet, by Sandra Cabot. Cobbitty: WHAS, 1996. Excellent, detailed detox one-month program.

One Minute Millionaire: The Enlightened Way to Wealth, by Mark Victor Hansen & Robert G. Allen. New York: Harmony Books, 2002 – www.money-millionaire.com

Rich Dad, Poor Dad, by Robert Kiyosaki with Sharon L. Lechter. Paradise Valley: Arizona.: Tech Press, 1997.

The Present: *The gift that makes you happy and successful at work and in life*, by Spencer Johnson. New York: Random House Inc, 2003.

The Purpose Driven Life: What on earth am I here for? by Rick Warren. Michigan: Zondervan, 2002.

The Richest Man in Babylon, by George S. Clason. New York: Penguin Group, 1955.

The Ultimate Weight Solution: *The 7 Keys to Weight Loss Freedom*, by Phil McGraw. New York: Free Press, 2003.

Take Time for Your Life, by Cheryl Richardson. New York: Broadway Books, 1999.

The Aladdin Factor: *How to ask for and get anything you want in life*, by Jack Canfield and Mark Victor Hansen. New York: Berkley, 1995.

The Cash Flow Quadrant: *Rich Dad's Guide to Freedom*, by Robert Kiyosaki and Sharon Lechter. Arizona: TechPress Inc, 1998.

The Little Book of Dreams, by Joan Hanger. Victoria: Penguin Books, 1998.

The Little Book of Sleep, by Paul Wilson. Victoria: Penguin Books, 1999.

The Mind Map Book: How to Use Radiant Thinking to Maximise Your Brain's Untapped Potential, by Tony Buzan and Barry Buzan. New York: Penguin Plume, 1996.

The Success Principles: *How to get from where you are to where you want to be*, by Jack Canfield with Janet Switzer. New York: Harper Collins Publishers, 2005.

Think and Grow Rich, by Napoleon Hill. New York: Fawcett Crest, 1960.

Ready, Set, Goal, by Wendy Buckingham. Frenchs Forest: Pearson Education Australia Pty Ltd, 2002.

Smart Couples' Guide to Money, by Gay Curtis and Simone Tregeagle. Sydney: Wrightbooks, 2004.

Smart Girls' Guide to Money, by Gay Curtis and Simone Tregeagle. Sydney: Wrightbooks, 2003.

Touch the Sky, by Patrick William Moore. McMahons Point: Way Books. 2002.

Win the Fat War, by Anne Alexander. Victoria: The Five Mile Press. 2000.

Would you Like Attitude With That? by Justin Herald, Crows Nest: Allen & Unwin, 2003.

Magazines

Cooking Pleasures Magazine. Official publication of the Cooking Club of America – www.cookingclub.com

Delicious Magazine. Produced by ABC magazines. Won magazine of the Year in 2003. Excellent, tasty recipes made from fresh Australian produce – www.fpc.com.au

Dumbo Feather, pass it on, Produced by Bezar Holdings Pty Ltd – www.dumbofeather.com

O, The Oprah Magazine produced by Harpo Productions Inc. This is my most favourite magazine – www2.oprah.com

Ezines

Great Speaking newsletter by Tom Antion. Great source of tips for anyone who presents in their role. Subscribe at www.antion.com

Food Lovers Workshop – unlocking the keys to health and vitality and loving every bite of it by Sherry Clewlow. Based in Melbourne, Australia, Sherry is a world leader in this area – her monthly newsletter is excellent. Subscribe at www.sherryclewlow.com

Websites

Activate Your Life Program – a fantastic three-month program designed to focus on your health and wellbeing – www.activateyourlife.com.au

Athlete's Foot – excellent Australian retailer for correctly fitting walking/running shoes using a Fitprint system – www.athletesfoot.com.au

Donna Jones, Fitness Editor, *Good Medicine* magazine, personal trainer and consultant – her new book, 'Workouts for Everyone' is fantastic – check it out at – www.donnajones.com.au

Fitness First Australia – www.fitnessfirst.com.au – great, well equipped gyms with a variety of machines, weights, cardio and classes.

Oprah Book Club – great source for recommended reading – www2.oprah.com

Mother Inc. – If you are a mum this site is a must for you. It is full of tips, ideas and an online glossy editorial created by Claudia Keech, Founder and CEO – fantastic resource for all working mums – www.motherinc.com.au

DVDs

Gaiam Yoga with Rodney Yee – easy to use, doesn't require expensive equipment and times vary from 15 minutes to 45 minutes – www.gaiam.com

Also by Neen James:

Books:

Network or Perish: Learn the secrets of master networkers
Balance: Real-Life Strategies for Work/Life Balance

CD packs:

How to Achieve Amazing Things in Your Work Life

How to Run a Successful Home-Based Business, by Neen James & Robyn Henderson

Find Your Market. How to find hot markets and responsive customers - CD pack by Gihan Perera with Neen James. Perth: The Step Up Series, 2005 - www.gihanperera.com

Get More Done: How to become massively productive and get on with it, by Neen James & Matt Church

Newsletter:

Subscribe to Neen's newsletter at www.neenjames.com

Neen is available for keynote speaking and training workshops to help your organisation boost its productivity – so that everyone can get more done. Book through your favourite speakers bureau or at **www.neenjames.com**.